Garden Getaways

# GARDEN GETAWAYS

## Public Gardens & Special Nurseries

## Northern California

NONA P. PIERCE

Photographs by Jimmie Pierce

Foreword by George Waters

**Tioga Publishing Company**
*Palo Alto, California*

*Library of Congress
Cataloging in Publication Data*

Pierce, Nona P., 1929–
Garden getaways :
public gardens and special nurseries
in northern California
*Nona P. Pierce.*
176 p. cm.
Includes index.

ISBN 0-935382-70-4

1. Gardens — California, Northern
— Guide-books.
2. Nurseries (Horticulture) — California,
Northern — Guide-books.
3. California, Northern — Description
and travel — Guide-books. I. Title.
SB466.U65C27 1989
712′ .09794 — dc 19

Acknowledgements:
Page 11: Reprinted by permission of the Luther Burbank Home & Gardens, Santa Rosa.
Page 56: Reprinted by permission of the John Muir Papers, Holt-Atherton Pacific Centers for Western Studies, University of the Pacific, copyright © 1984 Muir-Hanna Trust.

Tioga Publishing Company
Box 50490
Palo Alto, CA 94303

Cover photograph of Filoli
by Charles Kennard
Illustrations by Mimi Osborne
Designed and produced
by Jon Goodchild/Triad
Typeset by TBD Typography

Printed in USA

# Contents

## 3. San Jose/South Bay



## 4. Santa Cruz/Monterey Bay



## 5. Central Valley/Gold Country

# Foreword

Garden visiting has a long and honorable history. Thomas Jefferson, his ideas for a garden at Monticello already well developed, in 1786 embarked upon a celebrated tour of English gardens in company with John Adams. Celia Fiennes, the earliest of several dedicated tourists, including Cobbett and Defoe, traveled Britain between 1686 and 1705, recording in gossipy detail her visits to the gardens of the great. Edith Wharton visited the villas and gardens of Italy in the late nineteenth century, seeing them as sources of instruction and inspiration for her writing on design and decoration, as one might also use museums and art galleries.

Garden styles have changed enormously since Jefferson and Fiennes — and even since Wharton's Victorian days — but gardeners have not. They still want to see what others have done, perhaps picking up a few ideas for their own gardens, and they still gossip about the successes and failures they find. As for study of the history of gardens, it has never been pursued with greater energy than now. But most of us visit gardens simply because of the pleasure it gives. Large or small, a well kept garden on a bright spring day is, as the doggerel reminds us, as close to heaven as earth allows.

Here in Northern California there are a great many gardens to see. They are so varied that, even if your visits are of the most casual kind, prompted by nothing but idle curiosity, you are sure to wonder at the differences among gardens: simple and formal; woodsy and natural; vaguely or explicitly oriental and deeply personal; showy and extrovert. Some are collections of fascinating plants maintained with care and patience; others are designs of great artistry in which plants are secondary to the plan. The differences derive in large part from the gardener, but there are other influences.

In its short history California has brought almost every nation to its shore, and gardening traditions from the Mediterranean, Asia, and especially Europe, all have left their mark here. From the early days of European settlement, our climate allowed the cultivation of plants from all corners of the earth, and immigrants made splendid gardens resembling those they had known in their homelands. The plants they chose also were favorites from home — some they had brought with them as seeds and slips — and many needed water year round to flourish. Keeping water flowing to thirsty plants throughout our rainless summers has always called for great effort and ingenuity, from buckets and wells to massive state water projects to the development, in recent years, of automatic irrigation gadgets.

People have been moving to California in increasing numbers, industry has spread, and the places where our wildflowers grow are being taken over for farming, buildings, and roads. Now we are cultivating wildflowers and other native plants in our gardens to avoid losing them entirely. At the same time it is becoming clear that as population increases, water supply does not; droughts every few years remind us of this. Some of us make gardens that need little or no summer watering, and in them we shelter the native plants that might otherwise disappear from the countryside.

Today, as well as gardens inspired by those in Spain, Japan, Britain, Scandinavia, Africa, and many other countries and cultures, we find gardens that respond to the need for conservation and the desire to preserve what Nature, in departing for less rapacious realms, has left behind. In addition, each garden reflects the idiosyncrasies of its creator. From all these sources of diversity an enormous variety of gardens has emerged, and visiting them helps us to appreciate gardening, in the phrase of a dear friend, "as a science, an art, and a source of joy."

George Waters, Editor
*Pacific Horticulture*

# Author's Note

A climbing hydrangea on a brick wall at Filoli was the seed idea for this book. I was so charmed by the unusual, lacy vine and the formal gardens of the beautiful estate near Woodside that I wondered what other intriguing plants and gardens there were to discover. Then a trip to Western Hills Rare Plant Nursery in Occidental brought further wonderment: such a wide variety, so many unusual plants, unknown to me. I wanted to tell others of the beautiful places and plants I was discovering.

I asked gardener friends if they knew about these gardens. Some did, and some didn't. Those who did not asked where they were and how they could get there. Following a visit to Santa Rosa, I inquired of these and other friends if they knew of Luther Burbank's gardens and that one of his original greenhouses still stands.

Or if they had seen a native plant arboretum in Carmel named for Lester Rowntree, the plantswoman who trekked through California in the 1930s and 1940s collecting seeds and plants, then urged gardeners to use them in their home landscapes. So it went; the more gardens I visited, the more I heard or read about. Slowly, conviction came that a guide book was the way to share my discoveries with others.

Some of the most pleasurable and most exhausting months of my life followed as I collected material for this book. It was about the usual gestation time: almost nine months of visits to dozens and dozens of gardens and special nurseries. As I strolled, sniffed, observed, took notes, and asked questions, my husband shared and recorded the beauty, taking hundreds of photographs.

I was thrilled to walk in conservationist John Muir's garden. I was honored to meet octogenarian Gerda Isenberg at her native plant nursery as she set out plants the day after her birthday. She takes scant notice of birthdays, however; her concern is that her land and garden be preserved after she is gone. And I was deeply impressed on a drizzly day as I wandered through Hakone Japanese Garden, sharply aware of the subtle textures and forms and the interplay of plants, rocks, water, and sky. It was with gratitude that I accepted a portion of Louis Saso's vast knowledge of the useful properties of herbs as he left his work to guide us through his garden.

After visiting more than one hundred sites, I appreciated the creativity and dedication of gardeners, designers, and owners of old estates and the volunteers who help them care diligently for gardens we enjoy today. I applauded those who preserved and protect historical sites and those who created and maintain our fine arboretums and botanical gardens. Friendly and helpful nursery owners and staff filled me with their enthusiasm for plants and impressed me with their eagerness to assist gardeners.

Of the many gardens and nurseries visited, those finally included in this book are open to the public; have horticultural merit, featuring unusual, rare, or comprehensive plant collections; have educational value, including good design, mature, labeled plants, and knowledgeable, helpful staff; demonstrate environmental sensitivity–especially with regard to conservation of natural resources, including low water use and use of native plants; and, perhaps most important, provide opportunities for an enjoyable outing for those who love plants and gardens. Selection was not easy, however, and I may have missed some important gardens and nurseries. If so, I hope readers will tell me about them.

Special thanks are due to Karen Nilsson, my publisher, for the talented, creative people she brought to this project, and for faith when I wanted to retreat. Thanks also to editor Nora Harlow, for high standards, respect, and for doing a difficult job with grace and humor. My appreciation goes to designer Jon Goodchild, for superb creative vision and for bringing it all together; and to artist Mimi Osborne, for inspiration and talent beautifully expressed. Agents Marjorie Gersh and Bill Oliver initiated the process and provided insight and good advice.

Most of all, thank you, Jimmie Pierce, for love and support, for beautiful photographs, for driving patiently and willingly to so many parts of Northern California, for teaching me that computers are not monsters, and for being absolutely indispensable to the project. This book would not have been possible without you.

Nona Pierce
Aptos, California, *January 1989*

# San Francisco/Peninsula

# 1.

# Strybing Arboretum

❀ Ninth Avenue at Lincoln Way, San Francisco

Strybing Arboretum and Botanical Gardens, on seventy acres of former sand dunes in Golden Gate Park, displays a multitude of plants that can be grown in the Bay Area's mild-winter climate. In this garden are over 6,000 plants from Mediterranean, temperate, and tropical areas of Asia, Central and South America, Australia, New Zealand, southern Europe, and Africa, as well as native California plants. Plants are grown in both geographic and specialized collections, and most are labeled. In ongoing renovation of the arboretum plants are grouped within regional areas by landscape use and cultural requirements. Combining plants in attractive masses rather than as botanical specimens gives visitors a sense of how plants can be used in home landscape designs.

Like an old friend seen from time to time, Strybing Arboretum is always changing, always the same. New collections are being developed, while older sections are being renovated. Wide terraces, seats, and rock walls invite visitors to pause and enjoy the Cape Province section, developed in 1985. There are many sun-loving plants from southern Africa, including silver trees (*Leucadendron argenteum*), heathers, and many bulbs. The New

*Cherry tree, magnolia, and bamboo complete picturesque scene*

World Cloud Forest, with plants from the mountains of southern Mexico and Central America, many of them endangered in their native habitats, was recently established in an area of old cypresses. As the old trees die, they will be replaced by three trees characteristic of the New World Cloud Forest: a rare magnolia (*Magnolia sharpii*), an oak (*Quercus pedunculosa*), and a pine (*Pinus pseudostrobus*). The understory includes fuchsias, abelias, and other tropical plants, some familiar to Bay Area gardeners.

One of the most outstanding of the Asiatic magnolias is the Campbell magnolia, a deciduous tree sixty to eighty feet tall, forty feet wide at maturity, with magnificent, rose-pink, bowl-like flowers up to ten inches across. There are more than twenty of these trees in the arboretum; visit in mid-winter to see them in flower. Most of the other magnolias are in bloom by March.

There are also superb collections of conifers and dwarf conifers, succulents, and rhododendrons, including tropical vireyas, in bloom from November to April. Over 200 camellias are in flower in early spring. Special gardens include a small, Japanese-style moon-viewing garden; the recently renovated Arthur Menzies Garden of California Native Plants, with a good selection of manzanitas, ceanothus, and other native plants; a redwood trail with trees, shrubs, and ferns of the state's foggy coastal canyons; a garden of fragrance with aromatic plants spilling over rock walls and labels in braille for the visually impaired; a biblical garden of plants with biblical references; and a demonstration garden with changing exhibits of colorful plants to inspire home gardeners. There is so much to see in this exceptional arboretum that a single visit only whets the appetite for more.

**Getting There:** Lincoln Way defines the southern boundary of Golden Gate Park. From Lincoln turn into park at Ninth Avenue. Arboretum is immediately on left. Park on street or in lot at nearby Music Concourse.

**Admission:** Free. Donations accepted at Strybing Store. Open weekdays 8am to 4:30pm; Saturday, Sunday, and holidays 10am to 5pm.

**Facilities:** Benches, drinking fountains, restrooms, fine horticultural library (open 10am to 4pm daily), store with books, gifts, cards, maps. Handicapped access generally good. Tours 1:30pm on weekdays; 10:30am and 1:30pm on weekends. Annual plant sale in May; smaller sales alternate Saturdays. Lectures, classes, field trips throughout the year. Call (415) 661-1316.

**Nearby:** Near Strybing Arboretum are Japanese Tea Garden; Asian Art and M.H. de Young Memorial museums; Rhododendron Dell; California Academy of Sciences; Shakespeare Garden; and Conservatory of Flowers, a Victorian glass house with tropical plants and seasonal floral displays. Near conservatory are collections of fuchsias, dahlias, and camellias.

# Japanese Tea Garden

❀ Hagiwara Tea Garden Drive, San Francisco

A legacy of the Midwinter Fair of 1894, which was designed to stimulate the city's recovery from the 1893 depression, the five-acre Japanese Tea Garden is one of the most popular attractions in Golden Gate Park.

Entry is through a gate constructed of hinoki cypress in 1985 by Japanese artisans. The landscape rises to a hilltop through a series of winding paths, across footbridges over ponds and streams, and up steps and ramps.

The Japanese-style landscape features many pruned cypresses and pines, small and large, nestled against rocks or arching over ponds where realistic bronze cranes stand as if waiting to spear fish. March and April are the best months to see many spectacular

*Azaleas and stone lantern at pool's edge*

camellias, azaleas, and cherry trees in bloom.

Bamboo fences, bamboo pruned as shrubs, and marble bamboo (*Chimonobambusa marmorea*) trimmed as low hedges are recurring elements in the garden, as are stone lanterns and mounds covered with low shrubs that alternately hide and reveal ponds behind them.

Paths lead past an unusually steep, arched, wooden bridge (called a drum bridge by Japanese), then uphill to the highest point in the garden, reached by a path or a steep flight of steps, to a red-orange temple gate and a many-tiered pagoda with a thin spire on top. Finely pruned cypresses, cedars, junipers, pines, azaleas, and red-leaf Japanese maples cover the hillside.

At the top is a clearing with beautiful views. The focus of the hilltop landscape is the red-orange pagoda surrounded by weathered wood fences and large hinoki cypresses in enormous pots on either side of wooden gates. Pruned Japanese sugi (*Cryptomeria japonica* 'Elegans') along the fence, tall clumps of heavenly bamboo (*Nandina domestica*, not a bamboo), and a graveled area with artfully placed rocks around the shrine add to the solemn mood.

A long bridge leads to a large bronze Buddha near the teahouse and gift shop, which are built of wood in Japanese architectural style. A counter with small stools in the teahouse overlooks a koi pond — a fine place to have tea and cookies and watch the fish. From the teahouse a path winds between Japanese maples that create a leafy tunnel. Note the cherry tree branch trained on a bamboo rail over a path.

There are many memorable views: benches by tranquil ponds, fine maple leaves and bamboo against sturdy rocks, rustic bridges, waterfalls tumbling down rocky gulches. Despite the crowds that often fill this special garden, it is a quiet respite from the city's clamor.

**Getting There:** Drive into Golden Gate Park onto Martin Luther King Drive to Hagiwara Tea Garden Drive. Park near Music Concourse.

**Admission:** Adults, $2; seniors and children 6 to 12, $1; ages 5 and under, free. Free major holidays and first Wednesday of month. Open 9am to 6:30pm daily March to October; 8:30am to 5:30pm in winter.

**Facilities:** Restrooms, gift shop, teahouse. Handicapped access limited.

**Nearby:** Golden Gate Park has many horticultural attractions, including Strybing Arboretum, Conservatory of Flowers, Rhododendron Dell, and Shakespeare Garden. Asian Art and de Young museums are adjacent to tea garden, and California Academy of Sciences (with aquarium and planetarium) is across the Music Concourse.

# Grace Marchant Garden

❀ Filbert and Sansome Streets, San Francisco

On the eastern slope of Telegraph Hill, beneath Coit Tower, is a two-acre hillside garden lovingly maintained by local residents. Grace Marchant, a retired Hollywood stuntswoman for whom this small paradise is now named, was responsible for its creation. When she moved into one of the picturesque hillside cottages dating from Gold Rush days a vacant lot outside her windows was heaped with accumulated trash. The rocky land gradually was cleared, and she began a garden.

Marchant worked tirelessly for thirty-three years until her death in 1982 at age ninety-six. In later years the heavy tasks were taken over by a younger neighbor, Gary Kray, who is still in charge of the garden.

The garden starts at Filbert Street at the base of Telegraph Hill and continues up to Coit Tower along wood and concrete steps, which also provide access to entry gardens of apartments and cottages on the hill. Each stair landing has a spectacular view of San Francisco Bay and the Bay Bridge.

When development was proposed for the garden area, residents convinced the city that the land should become a public trust.

*Cat stands sentry on hillside steps*

Funds were raised by selling "title" to the garden in square inches to hundreds of contributors. The cottage-style oasis in an otherwise urban landscape is a refreshing model for other cities, demonstrating how people can participate in the simple pleasures of neighborhood beautification through community effort.

A white arbor, a small bench, wisteria vines, hydrangeas, roses, and a sign reading "Time Began in a Garden" are found in a tangle of foliage and flowers. At Napier Lane the wooden steps expand into a deck. A community bulletin board is here, and there are exceptional views of Treasure Island and the Bay Bridge. A narrow alley runs between cottages where cats sprawl and lurk, watching for unwary birds.

Petunias, geraniums, and nicotiana ramble over the slope. Many roses, including the fragrant 'Cécile Brunner,' grow in a sunny clearing. Sweet alyssum, baby's tears, and violets carpet the ground under shrubs and trees. Tulips, daffodils, and other bulbs push through to bloom in spring. Japanese maples and tulip trees do well here, and even lemon, apple, and peach trees seem to enjoy the cool breezes off the bay.

Angel's trumpet or datura (*Brugmansia*), large shrubs with tubular flowers especially fragrant at night, were donated by the city. Blue hibiscus (*Alyogyne huegelii*) and bougainvillea add striking colors; fuchsias and bottlebrushes attract hummingbirds. Rich, purple-red accents are provided by valerian, purple-leaf plum, and butterfly bush (*Buddleia*). Towering over all is a huge, old American elm tree. Wooden gates, picket fences, the fragrance of summer roses, and the winter glory of pyracantha berries and camellias all contribute to this once cluttered hillside transformed into a joyous garden.

**Getting There:** Van Ness Avenue (Highway 101) to Bay Street. Turn east and continue to the Embarcadero; turn right then right again on Battery Street, then right on Greenwich. Park on street or in public lot at Sansome and Greenwich. Steps begin at Filbert Street at base of Telegraph Hill next to Levi Plaza.

**Admission:** Free. Open daily.

**Facilities:** Benches. No handicapped access.

**Nearby:** Restaurants at end of Montgomery Street, about half-way up stairs. Coit Tower is famed for murals painted by WPA artists and superb views. At bottom of steps, near Filbert and Sansome, are shops and eating establishments. A few blocks west is Pier 39, with restaurants and shops, and at end of Hyde Street is Fisherman's Wharf and Maritime Park, where the sailing ship, Balclutha, is anchored.

# Acres of Orchids

❀ 1450 El Camino Real, South San Francisco

A few miles from San Francisco's busy international airport and only fifteen minutes from the city is a fabulous array of exotic orchids. With 800,000 square feet of greenhouses, Rod McLellan's orchid nursery is one of the largest in the world.

New orchids are hybridized each year, and old favorites are propagated for a world-wide market. McLellan's orchids have won numerous awards in international shows. Although the nursery does not specialize in a particular kind of orchid, moth orchids (*Phalaenopsis*) are a favorite of home growers because these are among the easiest to grow. They do well at room temperature and thrive in low light. Flowers last up to two months, and some plants bloom several times a year. They are available in bud from December to May.

Cattleya orchids, used in corsages, are another favorite. Left on the plant, the large flowers have a subtle yet luxuriant fragrance and last for several weeks. Plants in bud are in abundant supply from March through May and August through October.

Tours of the laboratory and greenhouses give visitors behind-the-scenes glimpses of the propagation of orchids by seed or by

*Delicate flowers of epiphytic moth orchid*

tissue culture, in which plants are grown from single cells in a sterile environment. Visitors also learn about the many varieties of orchids that are available and how budded plants are prepared for shipping so they will bloom on cue for special occasions.

In addition to orchids, the nursery has an enormous greenhouse area and offers many gardenias, sprays of dyed and preserved eucalyptus leaves, and a wide selection of house plants. The orchid sales house features a tropical garden with waterfall and many unusual plants on display. Everything needed for growing, potting, and caring for orchids is also for sale. A catalog with beautiful color illustrations helps customers select the right plants.

Surely Edgar McLellan, son of a Gold Rush pioneer and dairy farmer, could not have envisioned such a large and diverse operation when he expanded a green-thumb hobby into a full-time nursery business in the late 1890s. His son, Rod McLellan, continues the family business under the fitting name of Acres of Orchids.

**Getting There:** Highway 280 to Hickey Boulevard exit east to El Camino Real (Highway 82); turn right one block and watch for nursery sign. Or Highway 101 to Highway 380 exit west to Highway 280 north to Hickey Boulevard exit east to El Camino Real. Park in lot.

**Admission:** Open 8am to 5pm, except major holidays.

**Facilities:** Restrooms. Handicapped access excellent. Sales house and gift shop. Monthly clinics on growing orchids. Free tours daily 10:30am and 1:30pm. For groups larger than five call (415) 871-5655.

**Nearby:** Pacific Orchids, a nursery offering tropical orchids that do well in the Bay Area, is on Station Avenue in Daly City; it is open by appointment only. Shelldance Bromeliads is on Highway 1 in Pacifica.

# Central Park Japanese Garden

❀ East Fifth Avenue, San Mateo

Tall buildings with window walls tower over this garden in busy downtown San Mateo, but on the quiet paths the feeling is serene. The Japanese garden is part of San Mateo's oldest park, known for its fine mature trees and colorful flowers.

Large native oaks, incorporated into the Japanese garden's design, mark the entry and blend with a variety of trees on the perimeter. A centrally located pond is divided by a narrow neck spanned by a bridge. A smaller, curved bridge with carved post caps connects the path to an island planted with variegated mugho pines, junipers, and Japanese red pines.

Azaleas and camellias along paths and at pond's edge are colorful accents in spring. Japanese apricots, cherries, and quince, purple-leaf plums, and magnolias add color from February to May.

A teahouse of smooth wood with a pleasant patina is circled by a rock-edged path. From comfortable benches here visitors enjoy the varied shapes and textures of pines, cypresses, oaks, and weeping cherries. Red-leaf Japanese maples add a lacy touch. Japanese koto music floats out from the teahouse.

On the other side of the pond is a five-story pagoda, a gift

*Tantalizing glimpse of garden through gable-roofed gate*

from the people of Toyonaka, Japan, San Mateo's sister city. This light-looking structure is actually a two-ton granite temple of divinities. Wisteria and ferns are a pleasing contrast to the stone pagoda. Nearby, the foliage of copper and purple beech trees stands out among pines and oaks. Red-leaf Japanese maples and purple-leaf plums grow beside a brook, from which a waterfall flows into a reflecting pool. Koi fish gather here in a frenzy at feeding time.

Artfully shaped trees and shrubs and others growing according to nature's design are blended into a harmonious whole. There are many noteworthy trees in the garden, including several varieties of beeches, weeping Japanese apricots, Camperdown elms, red horsechestnuts, and bristlecone pines. Look for the tri-color beech, with light green leaves edged with pink, overhanging a path.

Jasmine wafts fragrance beside steps up to a small pavilion, seemingly enclosed by a grove of black bamboo and Japanese cedars. There are benches inside and a map of the garden with major trees and shrubs identified.

**Getting There:** Highway 101 to San Mateo; take East Third Avenue exit and go west to El Camino Real (Highway 82). Turn left, then left again at Fifth Avenue. Park in nearby underground parking garage.

**Admission:** Free. Open Monday to Friday 8:30am to 4pm; Saturday, Sunday, and holidays 11am to 5pm.

**Facilities:** Benches, drinking fountain. Restrooms in adjacent community center. Handicapped access excellent. Central Park has tennis courts, ball fields, playgrounds, and picnic tables. Fish feeding 11am and 3pm. Teahouse open for viewing 11am to 5pm, summer only. For information call (415) 377-4700.

**Nearby:** Peters & Wilson Nursery, specializing in unusual conifers, Japanese maples, and rhododendrons, is on Rollins Road in Millbrae.

# Filoli

❀ Cañada Road, Woodside

Set among rolling hills twenty-five miles south of San Francisco, Filoli, an English-style Georgian manor house designed by Willis Polk for Mr. and Mrs. William Bourn, Jr., in the early 1900s, has one of the most elegant gardens in Northern California.

Bourn, owner of the Empire Gold Mine near Grass Valley, chose the site because it reminded him of the Lakes of Killarney in Ireland. The name Filoli was created from the first two letters of the words Fight, Love, and Live (Bourn's credo was "Fight for a just cause, love your fellow man, and live a good life.") The Bourns lived at Filoli until their deaths in 1936. Mr. and Mrs. William Roth purchased the property in 1937, and in 1975 Mrs. Roth deeded the house and 125 acres to the National Trust for Historic Preservation.

Seventeen acres of the large estate were developed into formal gardens, now mature, enhanced by loving care during the Roths' long stewardship. The landscape is a series of outdoor rooms. Clouds of white clematis, purple wisteria, and deciduous magnolias in the gravel entry court bloom gloriously in spring. Coast live oaks, 300 to 500 years old, and columnar Irish yews, regularly pruned to maintain their shape, are frame and background to the gardens.

In summer yellow 'Lady Banks' roses cascade over walls, wisteria billows over stone balustrades, and plumbago blooms in blue drifts near terraces next to the house, which look out over fields and woods. Brick steps lead to a sunken garden and serene pool reflecting the sky with pots of Japanese irises and clipped bush germanders as corner accents. Behind the swimming pool is a 'Sunburst' honey locust (*Gleditsia triacanthos*), a pleasantly unruly contrast with precise flower beds in the foreground.

Symmetrical beds in the walled garden are filled with spring bulbs and summer annuals. In the Chartres Cathedral window garden tree roses are interspersed with fat mounds of pruned boxwood. Beyond the walled garden are the panel gardens, where borders are filled with deep blue Chinese forget-me-nots and the path is lined with hundreds of bearded irises, resplendent in spring. Here also is the rose garden, fragrant and lush in summer with a succession of blooms from hundreds of bushes.

The sunny knot garden consists of plants with gray, soft green, and burgundy foliage. Dwarf lavender, santolina, hyssop, and red-leaf barberry are some of the plants growing here. A hedge of copper beech separates areas, and clipped hollies line paths to a fine collection of peonies, at peak bloom in mid-spring.

*Oaks and bright flowers set off English-style manor house*

The highest point of the garden is a grassy knoll with a long view down an allée of Irish yews. Wrought-iron gates in a brick wall lead to a camellia garden, which also has azaleas, rhododendrons, ferns, and other shade-loving plants. Dogwood trees are outstanding in bloom in early spring.

Camperdown elms with umbrella-shaped crowns of intricately twisted branches grow near the swimming pool. The view from this pleasant entertainment area, with large patio protected by rows of tall yews on either side of the pool, is dominated by the carriage house clock tower. A climbing hydrangea (*Hydrangea anomala*) grows on a nearby wall.

Knowledgeable visitors from around the world are impressed by the variety of plants at Filoli and the exceptional quality of maintenance, augmented by over seventy volunteer gardeners.

**Getting There:** Highway 280 to Edgewood Road exit west to Cañada Road. Turn right and go about a mile to gatehouse on left. Park in lot. Tours start here.

**Admission:** Tours, $6, mid-February to mid-November Tuesday through Saturday. Reservations required (415) 364-2880. No one under 12 admitted.

**Facilities:** Restrooms, drinking fountains, benches, tea room. No picnicking. Tours ending with box lunches for large groups may be arranged. Some plants and books for sale in garden shop. Handicapped access limited; call for special arrangements. Nature hikes through wilder parts of estate by reservation; group hikes can be arranged.

# Yerba Buena Nursery

❀ 19500 Skyline Boulevard, Woodside

This four-acre nursery, started by Gerda Isenberg in the 1950s, offers more than 350 kinds of plants native to California, as well as a wide selection of ferns, both native and exotic. There is also a large demonstration garden, a long-term project still in progress, where visitors can see how plants will behave when removed from their nursery containers.

The farmhouse and barn were built in 1905, and Gerda is the second owner of the property. As were the original ranchers, she is a pioneer. It was her championing of native plants that established the nursery as an early and reliable source of hard-to-find California shrubs, trees, and perennials, especially drought-tolerant plants.

Although signs are helpful, the long drive on an unpaved road may discourage some visitors. The octogenarian owner, who still plants and tends the nursery and garden, says old-timers call first, especially in wet weather. The helpful staff and the abundance and quality of plants make it a rewarding trip.

The house, lath houses, greenhouses, potting shed, and office are set back from a ravine shaded by oaks and redwoods. There is a new fern house here, while down the slope are lath houses for hardier ferns. At least fifteen native and over forty exotic ferns are offered. Ideal conditions along the rock-walled path encourage bleeding heart, sorrel, large ferns, and other shade plants.

The demonstration garden, which takes up about half the acreage, is in a bowl-like hollow with benches on each side overlooking the garden. Mown grass paths between labeled plants allow one to learn while strolling. Some plants are in wire cages to protect them from browsing deer, but most are left unprotected so visitors can assess suitability for their own gardens.

Rabbits, quail, and song birds find cover in thickets on the edge of the demonstration area. There are many kinds of manzanita and ceanothus, including *Ceanothus* 'Gerda Isenberg,' a large shrub behind a bench on the east slope above the garden. This is a good place to view the contrasting growth habits, textures, and colors of plants in the sunny meadow below.

Native ferns, penstemons, bush monkeyflower, and red-flowering currant are some of the plants here. Island bush poppy, with clear, yellow flowers, and Cleveland sage, a tall plant with striking, blue-purple flowers, are especially attractive in bloom. Of the many sages, perhaps the most dramatic is *Salvia apiana*, with fragrant white flowers on spikes over six feet tall and lemon-scented leaves said to be unpalatable to deer. A large stand of matilija poppies, with huge, yellow-centered, white flowers that resemble crepe paper, grows near an old shed. These plants, once established, need almost no water in summer.

The nursery offers most of the plants on display in the demonstration garden, including, in a recent catalog, six kinds of buckwheat, twenty-six kinds of ceanothus, eleven kinds of pines (including the slow-growing bristlecone), dozens of ferns, and seventeen manzanitas. This nursery is an ideal place to see what mature native plants will look like before you purchase them for your own garden.

**Getting There:** Highway 280 to Highway 84 (Woodside Road) west. Take Skyline Boulevard (Highway 35) south and go about 4.5 miles. Turn right on Rapley Ranch Road at nursery sign onto dirt and gravel road. Continue, mostly downhill, about two miles to nursery. Watch for signs. Park in front of fern house.

**Admission:** Open daily 9am to 5pm, except major holidays.

**Facilities:** Restrooms, benches, demonstration garden. Paths unpaved, but nursery premises and restrooms designed for handicapped access. Call (415) 851-1668.

**Nearby:** Woodside Library, on Woodside Road, has a garden featuring mature native and drought-tolerant plants.

# Sunset Magazine

❀ Willow and Middlefield Roads, Menlo Park

If ever there were a shrine for western gardeners, the headquarters of *Sunset*, "The Magazine of Western Living," certainly would be at the top of the list. On the seven-acre site, once part of the Rancho de las Pulgas land grant of 1815, are adobe office buildings designed in 1951 by Cliff May, who popularized the informal, open, ranch-house style of western architecture.

The property backs up to San Francisquito Creek, where coast live oaks, buckeyes, big-leaf maples, bay laurels, Douglas firs, and coast redwoods form a sheltering backdrop for the garden designed by Thomas Church. The high windows of the entrance lobby look out on an impressive display of flowering shrubs and trees surrounding several panels of lawn. Turf areas in front of the building were replaced during the 1988 drought with several varieties of drought-resistant grasses, ivy, juniper, and other ground-hugging plants requiring as little as one-tenth of the water the lawns demanded in the past. Although water use has been cut back considerably, Sunset does not expect to abandon its spectacular seasonal floral displays, which attract hundreds of tourists and garden lovers every year.

*Bedding plants enliven oak-shaded paths*

Permanent plantings include specimen coast live oaks and valley oaks, as well as plants native to or widely grown on the Pacific coast, from the Northwest to the deserts of Southern California. In a shady garden are rhododendrons, azaleas, camellias, ferns, dogwoods, western redbuds, huckleberries, and mahonias, along with California buckeyes, vine maples, bay laurels, and Japanese maples. Douglas firs on the perimeter shade and protect other plants from wind.

Along with seasonal bedding plants, the layering of plants of different sizes, textures, and colors and the use of native plants alongside cultivated exotics are common practices at Sunset. Raised beds and a variety of flowers, shrubs, and trees in novel pots and planters are also Sunset ideas that have gained wide acceptance.

Tile pavers and a central rectangular pool with water jet under an old olive tree give a mission-era atmosphere to an enclosed court. Pots contain seasonal flowers — tulips, orchids, achilleas, ranunculus. Pansies, jonquils, primroses, and azaleas are colorful in beds in the spring sun.

Under the outstretched arms of a stone statue of St. Francis is an area of dwarf citrus, where the technique of espaliering lemon trees on a low fence can be studied. Other dwarf citrus are Washington and Robertson navels, Valencia oranges, Marsh seedless and ruby-red grapefruits, and Dancy tangerines.

Whatever your horticultural interest you probably will find an example at Sunset headquarters — from roses and rhododendrons to oranges and oaks — in a gracious setting, with knowledgeable people to guide you.

**Getting There:** Highway 101 to Menlo Park; take Willow Road exit west and go about a mile to Middlefield Road. Park on street or in lot.

**Admission:** Free. Open weekdays 8am to 4:30pm. Tours of building 10:30 and 11:30am and 1, 2, and 3pm. Walk through gardens anytime. Groups of eight or more should call in advance (415) 321-3600.

**Facilities:** Restrooms, benches. Handicapped access good.

**Nearby:** Allied Arts Guild, with shops and courtyard gardens, is also in Menlo Park. Edgewood Park, with spring wildflowers in serpentine grassland, is on Stagecoach Road in Redwood City. Gamble Garden Center is in Palo Alto, and Stanford's Rodin Sculpture Garden is on the university campus.

# Allied Arts Guild

❀ 75 Arbor Road, Menlo Park

The Allied Arts Guild was established in the 1920s as a center for artists and craftspeople to work in a supportive, communal environment. The three-and-one-half-acre center today houses the studios and shops of potters, painters, weavers, jewelry and candle makers, needleworkers, and photographers in a charming Spanish-style complex with tile-roofed buildings, secluded courtyards, fountains, murals, and rustic wood gates and doors. Flowers in pots and beds are changed with the season, and inviting paths encourage visitors to explore.

The gardens are designed as a series of courtyards. A central Court of Abundance has a fountain with decorative tiles. Brick

*Sun-splashed path lined with roses and boxwood*

walks are bordered by boxwood hedges in half-circles and citrus trees. Beds of colorful annuals circle the fountain.

A two-story building containing several shops is landscaped with camellias, fuchsias, roses, and a large persimmon tree. Through a side gate brick walks lead behind this building to redwoods, persimmons, and Japanese cut-leaf maple trees. A long brick walk is lined with olive trees, hollies, and rows of tree roses bordered by low boxwood hedges. A wisteria-draped arbor gives entry to a hidden court where an old barn and sheds, retained from the nineteenth-century ranch on which the complex was established, have been made into shops and studios. A sheltering oak tree, quince, pomegranate, white-flowered oleander, and pots of succulents in the sun create a pleasing mix of textures and colors, shade and light. Hawthorn trees and heavenly bamboo are lacy and colorful against the aged redwood barn.

From a luncheon restaurant diners look out on a Garden of Delight, with tiled pool and fountain circled by brick walks, flower beds, and benches under tall shrubs. A patio off the restaurant, known as Cervantes Court, features a mural of Cervantes dedicating his masterpiece, *Don Quixote*. Tables here are set up under shady awnings, and hanging baskets and an island bed of flowers add bright colors. Many of the tiles and objects of art in the gardens were brought from Spain, Tunis, and Morocco; others were made by local artists.

The Allied Arts Guild benefits the Children's Hospital at Stanford. To raise funds, Woodside-Atherton Auxiliary volunteers initially served lunches made in their homes and brought to the guild. Volunteers now staff the restaurant, preparing food on site and serving thousands of visitors year round. Volunteers also staff the adjacent shop in which fine gifts, flower arrangements, and table settings are sold.

**Getting There:** Highway 101 to Embarcadero Road exit toward Palo Alto; turn right on El Camino Real, continue past Stanford shopping center to Cambridge, and turn left to Arbor Road. Or Highway 280 to Sand Hill Road exit toward Menlo Park; continue to El Camino Real, turn left, go to Cambridge, then turn left and continue to Arbor Road. Park in lot.

**Admission:** Shops open 9:30am to 5pm except Sunday. Restaurant open noon to 2pm for lunches or desserts. Reservations preferred. Call (415) 324-2588.

**Facilities:** Benches, tables, chairs, drinking fountains, restaurant, restrooms. Handicapped access good. In addition to arts and crafts stores, there are shops selling antiques, women's and children's clothing, gourmet cookware, and plants.

**Nearby:** Stanford's Rodin Sculpture Garden, Sunset magazine headquarters, and Gamble Garden Center are all nearby.

# Rodin Sculpture Garden

❀ Lomita Drive and Roth Way, Stanford

Visiting a sculpture garden may expand our ideas of what gardens can be. Although few homeowners will have a bronze figure by Rodin in the backyard, garden ornaments, fountains, pedestals with pots of cascading flowers — even plants themselves — can be used as sculpture in the landscape.

A wonderful place to contemplate some possibilities is the B. Gerald Cantor Sculpture Garden at Stanford University, with twenty bronze sculptures by Rodin set in the straightforward yet subtle design of landscape architect Robert Middelstadt. The garden was designed and plants selected to create the atmosphere of a French garden. The one-acre garden is divided diagonally by the placement of sculptures and a triangular bed of low-growing junipers. A free-form border is planted with a seasonally changing array of annuals. On a ten-foot column the Spirit of Eternal Repose, a tilting sculpture that seems to defy gravity, adds a shaft of audacity in the triangle of soft green junipers.

In the center of a terrace is a figure from the monument known as The Burghers of Calais, which illustrates the story of six French men who offered to give up their lives to the king of England to spare their town during the Hundred Years' War. Columnar Italian cypresses are spaced around the circle and beside the terrace outside the museum rotunda. The tall cypresses repeat the vertical thrust of the sculptures and evoke images of both sunny Italy and France, Rodin's homeland.

Sun and shadow are important elements of this garden, as seen in the enormous bronze Gates of Hell, set against a freestanding wall facing south. The passage of light plays over the intricately detailed surfaces. At top center is a representation of the inward-looking Thinker, set forward so the last light of day lingers on head and hand.

Circles are a recurrent motif. Facing the Gates of Hell on its circular, stage-like terrace are three circular concrete seats. Round planters beside the garden entrance repeat the circular theme, and perimeter trees and shrubs add a sense of enclosure. The Burgher of Calais also is set on a round terrace with an inset circle of brick. Steps into the museum at the end of the terrace lead to the B. Gerald Cantor Art Gallery with many small models of Rodin's work.

**Getting There:** Highway 101 in Palo Alto to University Avenue exit west (University changes to Palm Drive on entering campus). Follow Palm to Museum Way and turn right one block to museum. Or take Highway 280 to Sand Hill Road exit east toward Stanford shopping center; turn right on Arboretum Road and right again on Palm Drive to campus. Park on street.

**Admission:** Garden free; museum by donation. Open 10am to 5pm Tuesday through Friday; 1pm to 5pm Saturday and Sunday. Docent-led tours of indoor and outdoor Rodin collections 2pm Wednesday and Saturday. Call (415) 723-2842.

**Facilities:** Restrooms in museum, benches, picnic tables. Handicapped access good.

**Nearby:** On campus near Memorial Church are additional Rodin statues and modern sculptures. Gamble Garden Center is in Palo Alto; Sunset magazine headquarters and Allied Arts Guild, both with gardens, are in Menlo Park.

# Gamble Garden Center

❀ 1431 Waverley Street, Palo Alto

A house and garden in a quiet residential area are being transformed into a garden center named for Elizabeth F. Gamble, who left her property to the City of Palo Alto. Adjacent to the Palo Alto Lawn Bowling Club grounds and not far from the area of turn-of-the-century homes known as Professorville, Gamble House and its gardens are being restored by volunteer efforts and the contributions of construction and lighting firms, nursery people, and tree pruning services.

Resident horticulturist Scott Loosley was hired in 1987, and, with garden plans completed, work has proceeded under his direction since that time. Neglected trees have been pruned or removed with the help of members of the California Association of Arborists. Two large magnolias and several oaks have been beautifully pruned by tree-care personnel in training.

Old sheds and a lath house have been turned into meeting rooms, restrooms, storage for tools and garden equipment, and an office for the horticulturist. Parking lots, paths, an allée of flowering trees, a fountain, vegetable and flower beds, and an extensive rose garden are underway.

In addition to mature oaks and magnolias, plants saved from the old garden to become part of the new include camellias, Canary Island date palms, and wisterias in the garden behind the Victorian mansion. More than 1,000 tulip bulbs and many flats of blue pansies were planted near the wisteria, the combination making a spring sensation. Also saved were Australian pines or beefwood (*Casuarina stricta*) with soft, needle-like foliage and cones, and an old *Michelia figo*, called banana shrub because the flowers have a banana-like fragrance. An enormous oak near a teahouse shades a patio and picnic table. California pepper trees, tulip trees, persimmon, and a cockspur coral tree (*Erythrina crista-galli*) have also been retained.

Classes on landscaping, plants, flower arranging, and cooking are held regularly, and a children's gardening project taught by senior volunteers is headquartered here. There is a non-circulating library of garden books, seed catalogs, and other materials in the house. As renovation progresses with volunteer and professional help, the garden center is becoming the community resource envisioned by its founders.

**Getting There:** Highway 101 to Embarcadero Road exit; go toward Palo Alto and turn left on Waverley. Or Highway 280 to Page Mill Road exit toward Palo Alto; go to El Camino Real, turn north, then right at Embarcadero and right again on Waverley. Park in lot on Churchill Street.

**Admission:** Free. Gardens open daily. Office open weekdays 10am to 1pm.

**Facilities:** Restrooms, benches, drinking fountains, picnic table. Handicapped access good. Library, meeting rooms, classes, events, garden tours. For information call (415) 329-1356.

**Nearby:** Professorville, with turn-of-the-century homes, makes an interesting walking tour. Sunset magazine headquarters, with gardens, is in Menlo Park at Willow and Middlefield roads. Rodin Sculpture Garden is on the Stanford campus, and Allied Arts Guild, with garden and shops, is on Arbor Road in Menlo Park.

# Oakland/East Bay

# 2.

# Blake Garden

❀ 70 Rincon Road, Kensington

This secluded eleven-acre hillside garden in an affluent residential neighborhood has panoramic views and a fine collection of native and exotic plants.

The house was built in the 1920s by Anson and Anita Symmes Blake, both from prominent Bay Area families. Anita and her sister Mabel Symmes, then a student of landscape architecture at the University of California, Berkeley, planned and planted the original gardens. The property was deeded to the university in 1957, and in 1962 the landscape architecture department took over the garden's care and renovation. The house is now the official residence of the president of the university and is not open to the public.

The most formal part of the garden, across from the entrance

*Fragrant arbor frames view of sunny patio*

to the house, centers on a reflecting pool and vine-covered grotto framed by a double row of evergreen magnolias. Intimate gardens on either side of the pool recall the sisters' interest in Asian art. A shady garden on the north side and a sunny garden on the south feature ceramic oriental statues that seem to communicate across symmetrical paths. Azaleas, camellias, dogwoods, and Japanese maples in the mostly pink-flowering shady garden were over-arched by a gnarled old evergreen pear tree until it blew down recently in a storm. Conical Alberta spruces accent the south garden path, where marigolds, achilleas, gray-leaved santolina, Shasta daisies, and other sun-loving, mostly yellow-flowered plants thrive.

Small bridges span a creek in the ravine that drains the hillside. Ferns, gingers, hostas, cyclamens, and rhododendrons in this canyon are shaded by redwoods and picturesque coast live oaks.

On a west-facing slope behind the house are drought-tolerant plants, including Mediterranean, Australian, South African, and many California natives in rock-walled, terraced beds. A wide path circles a large lawn below the terraces, where an enormous oak shades a picnic table.

There is a large stand of rough-barked Canary Island pines and an oak woodland with cork oaks from Spain, pin oaks from the eastern United States, and daimyo oaks (*Quercus dentata*) from Korea, China, and Japan. Large beeches, an unusual Chilean tree near the house with large white flowers in summer (*Eucryphia* 'Nymansay'), Australian mimosa or silver wattle (*Acacia dealbata*) with silvery gray bark and leaves and scented flowers, and several kinds of magnolias are just a few of the garden's special trees.

A sunny, flat area south of the house features a square lily pond in a gravel court with tulip trees at each corner, a long arbor covered with flowering vines, and a raised pavilion with seats, often used for classes. A secluded bench offers a magnificent view across Berkeley to San Francisco Bay.

This compact but enormously varied garden has been sensitively restored for education, research, and enjoyment.

**Getting There:** Highway 80 in El Cerrito to San Pablo Avenue exit south; continue to Moeser and turn east toward hills. Continue uphill to Arlington Avenue, turn right, go to Rincon, and turn right again. Park in lot.

**Admission:** Free. Open weekdays 8am to 4:30pm. Closed legal holidays.

**Facilities:** Restrooms, benches, drinking fountain, picnic table. Handicapped access generally good, but some areas inaccessible by wheelchair. Group tours by appointment. Call (415) 524-2449 between noon and 1pm.

**Nearby:** University of California Botanical Garden and East Bay Regional Parks' Tilden Park Botanic Garden are both nearby in Berkeley.

# Berkeley Rose Garden

❀ 1201 Euclid Avenue, Berkeley

This secluded garden at the foot of Berkeley's Cordonices Park provides an unobstructed place to watch the sun set, with a spectacular view of the bay and Golden Gate Bridge. It is a quiet retreat, ideal for reading and relaxation.

WPA laborers tamed the slide-prone hillside in the early 1930s and built the stone steps and amphitheater designed by landscape architect V. M. Dean. Volunteers from local rose societies donated countless hours of planting time, and nurseries sold roses at a discount to start the garden during the depression.

A curving arbor over 200 feet long on the uppermost terrace is covered with climbing roses of many colors, including 'Joseph's Coat', with red-orange, gold, and pink-gold blooms on the same

*Rose-covered terraces look out to San Francisco Bay*

bush. This fragrant corridor of shifting light and shadow is lined with benches looking out to panoramic views. Rock-walled terraces step down the hill, where wide asphalt paths between raised beds allow visitors to enjoy more than 3,000 roses grown in planting blocks of one color interspersed with single bushes.

Swaths of yellow 'Sunbright' are planted along stone steps leading down to a pond and bridge at the bottom. 'Sally Holmes', with flat, pinkish white blooms like clustered bouquets of huge apple blossoms, grows across the path from 'Sweet Afton', a clear white, sweetly fragrant rose. Old moss roses grow near the creek, where paths lead to a naturalized area with oaks and redwoods. A bench by the pond gives a view up the slope and across the garden.

In a cooperative effort with the City of Berkeley, the Rose Society of Berkeley has a test garden area on the lower level, another example of the long-time community interest that continues to nurture this beautiful garden.

**Getting There:** Highway 80 to University Avenue exit in Berkeley. Go east on University to Oxford Street, turn left, and continue to Hearst Avenue. Turn right on Hearst, then left on Euclid. Park on street.

**Admission:** Open daily sunrise to sunset.

**Facilities:** Benches, drinking fountains. Handicapped access limited. Restrooms at tennis courts next to garden. Park has playfields, basketball courts, playground equipment. Fine view from above playing fields.

**Nearby:** University of California Botanical Garden is on Centennial Drive behind campus stadium. East Bay Regional Parks' Tilden Park Botanic Garden, devoted to native plants, is in hills above Berkeley on Wildcat Canyon Road, and Blake Garden is in nearby Kensington. Berkeley Horticultural Nursery is on McGee Avenue and Magic Gardens Nursery is on Heinz Avenue in Berkeley.

# Tilden Park Botanic Garden

❀ Wildcat Canyon Road, Berkeley

In the hills above Berkeley ten acres have been set aside for a botanic garden devoted to the display and preservation of the native plants of California. Newcomers to California, as well as long-time residents, will find the East Bay Regional Parks' Tilden Park Botanic Garden an enjoyable introduction to the beauty and diversity of plants from around the state. It is a walk through the varied California landscape in only a few hours.

The garden consists of ten sections and three subsections, from the cool Pacific rainforest to Southern California's semi-arid regions. Plant labels (a different color for each section) give the source of each plant. Plants in the Shasta-Cascade section, for example, include mountain-misery (*Chamaebatia foliolosa*) and

*A walk through the varied landscapes of California*

leopard lily (*Lilium pardalinum*). In the Sierran section a mature huckleberry oak from Lake Tahoe is a shrub rather than a tree.

Trails lead in several directions from the oak-shaded entrance. Comfortable benches on the visitors center terrace give a good overview of a ravine, slopes, creek, and pond. Down a path fragrant sweet shrub (*Calycanthus occidentalis*), which blooms for months, and Pacific dogwood, good for home gardens, grow beside a bridge spanning the creek. A clearing with a number of small ponds in a meadow dotted with quaking aspens is a lovely spot in the Sierran section. Narrow-leaf willows, from Mono County on the east side of the Sierra, grow beside a pond.

Winding paths lead along a ridge, down past coast silktassel, pines, and oaks to a grove of giant redwoods, then on down to shady Wildcat Creek. Tall Santa Lucia firs with drooping branches, and pallid manzanita (*Arctostaphylos pallida*), with wide-spreading, iron-red trunks and peeling bark, are outstanding along the hillside path.

Desert pinyon and Arizona cottonwood are just two of the many plants in the Sierra Madre area, where tiny lizards sun themselves on rocks beside wide stone paths.

There is year-round interest in this garden. The "most nearly complete collection of manzanitas and ceanothuses to be found anywhere," according to the garden's brochure, starts blooming in December and continues through spring into summer, along with many other native shrubs, perennials, and bulbs. In fall the leaves of deciduous trees change color and berries appear. With plants from throughout the state, including examples of all the conifers and nearly all the state's oaks, this garden is an impressive resource for both research and enjoyment.

**Getting There:** Highway 580 to Highway 24 east toward Walnut Creek; immediately through Caldecott Tunnel, take Fish Ranch Road exit, go uphill to Grizzly Peak Boulevard, and turn right toward Tilden Park. Follow Grizzly to South Park Drive, turn right, and go to intersection with Wildcat Canyon Road. Park in lot across road.

**Admission:** Free. Open daily 8:30am to 5pm, except major holidays.

**Facilities:** Restrooms, drinking fountains. Handicapped access generally good, but limited in some areas. Lectures, exhibits, slide shows, brochures at visitors center. Free tours June through August, Saturdays and Sundays 1:30pm. Group tours by appointment; call (415) 841-8732. Plant sale in April.

**Nearby:** Tilden Park has hiking and equestrian trails, golf course, tennis courts, lakes, swimming, picnic and camp areas, carousel and pony rides, miniature steam train, children's farm, and environmental education center.

# U.C. Botanical Garden

❀ Centennial Drive, Berkeley

The temperate Mediterranean climate of the San Francisco Bay area is ideal for one of the oldest college-associated botanical gardens in the United States. The thirty-three-acre garden was established in 1890, and its impressive collections are still expanding. Most of the garden is arranged by geographic region, with more than one-third of the area devoted to California natives. Many rare, endangered, and unusual plants grow in the varied terrain.

Just past the visitors center is the New World Desert, one of the oldest collections in the garden, with some plants dating to the 1930s. The gravelly soil on this sunny hillside is a perfect spot for a fascinating variety of cacti and succulents from deserts and mountains of the Americas. Opposite the New World Desert is the South African section with ice plants, euphorbs, lilies, and unusual aloes, especially attractive in spring bloom.

Wide paths lead to the shady Asian section, where Strawberry Creek is incorporated into the Japanese Garden. Here are a waterfall, lily pond, stone lanterns, irises, and a rhododendron dell with tree-like specimens brilliant in spring flower. Tall redwoods along the creek, coast live oaks, Italian stone pines, and other

*Cacti thrive on sunny slopes in gritty soil*

mature trees form a quiet woodland with an understory of unusual shrubs and herbaceous plants collected during expeditions in China.

The floriculture area at the far end of the path gives a wide view over canyons and hillsides and out to San Francisco Bay. A charming arbor with twining roses, rose beds interspersed with lavender and other flowers, and sweeping views from convenient benches make this a fragrant resting place.

In the Garden of Economic Plants—those used for cooking, fragrance, and medicinal purposes—and the Chinese Healing and Western Culinary Herb Gardens labels describe uses of the plants. Picnic tables under oak trees are nearby.

The California area, with many rare or endangered native plants, has an oak knoll, pygmy forest, raised beds with over 300 California native bulbs and corms, and a vernal pool—a transitory feature in boggy spring plains and meadows also known as "hog wallows." The scenic picnic area near the bulb beds is a good place to enjoy the spring flowers of lilies, amaryllids, and brodiaeas. A rewarding visit could be planned around this outstanding collection, the largest of its kind in California.

Also in the garden are a redwood grove with wildflowers, shrubs, and ferns found in coastal redwood forests, an Australian/New Zealand section with many drought-tolerant plants that do well in California's Mediterranean climate, sections with plants from South America, Mexico and Central America, and the eastern United States, and a collection of palms and cycads. Greenhouses hold tropical plants, insectivorous plants, and ferns.

**Getting There:** Highway 80 to Berkeley; take University Avenue exit east to Oxford Street and turn left. Go to Hearst Avenue, turn right, continue to Gayley Road, turn right, then left on Rim Road and left again on North Canyon Road. Entrance at curve where North Canyon Road meets Centennial Drive. Park in lot.

**Admission:** Free. Open daily 9am to 4:45pm, except Christmas.

**Facilities:** Restrooms, benches, drinking fountains, picnic tables. Handicapped access generally good. Visitors center store has books, cards, posters, some plants. Free tours of garden Saturday and Sunday 1:30pm. Classes, workshops throughout the year. Spring plant sale in May. Call (415) 642-3343.

**Nearby:** Continue on Centennial Drive to the university's Lawrence Hall of Science, with fascinating exhibits for all ages. East Bay Regional Parks' Tilden Park Botanic Garden, devoted to California native plants, is at Wildcat Canyon Road and South Park Drive. Blake Garden is nearby in Kensington.

# East Bay Garden Center

❀ 666 Bellevue Avenue, Oakland

Like a bed of flowers artfully combined, space at the Oakland-East Bay Garden Center on Lake Merritt is shared by sixty civic and garden clubs. Meeting rooms overlook a Japanese garden with teahouse and pool. Rhododendrons, azaleas, and bamboos are shaded by mature redwoods, coast live oaks, and Italian stone pines. Camellias and fuchsias thrive in the filtered light. Trial and test gardens dedicated to promoting knowledge of horticulture and enhancing the beauty of Oakland are planted and maintained by local plant societies. Most plants are labeled.

Volunteers help park department gardeners with planting and maintenance, and a continuous feast of flowering plants follows the seasons. Greenhouses shelter tropical and semi-tropical plants, including a banana tree with ripening stalks of fruit, gesneriads, bromeliads, and papyrus.

A garden sponsored by the East Bay Municipal Utility District demonstrates the use of composted sewage sludge with drought-tolerant plants and water-saving irrigation. Turf areas here are small, separated by dry, rock-filled stream beds. Mounds and beds contain rock roses, santolina, and herbs. A wisteria-covered

*Palms and banana trees lend a tropical air*

arbor leads to an information board describing this garden.

A fragrance and texture garden is a sensory experience, with spicy dill, mints, scented geraniums, and a gazebo adorned with sweet-smelling jasmine. Plant labels here are in braille.

Lake Merritt, the oldest man-made waterbird refuge in the United States, dating from 1870, is always in view from the gardens. Thousands of migratory birds visit, and the sounds of ducks, geese, and other birds are a pleasing accompaniment to a stroll in the gardens.

**Getting There:** Highway 880 to Broadway exit east; continue to Grand Avenue, turn right, then right on Bellevue Avenue. Park in lot.

**Admission:** Free, but $2 parking on weekends. Open Monday through Friday 10am to 3pm, Saturday and Sunday 10am to 5pm (4pm closing November through April). Closed major holidays. Horticultural library open Wednesday through Saturday 1 to 3 pm.

**Facilities:** Restrooms, benches, picnic tables. Handicapped access excellent. Plant sales in June and October. Flower shows throughout the year. To tour greenhouses, ask gardener to open doors or call for appointment (415) 273-3151.

**Nearby:** Walking and jogging the lakeside path are popular activities. Rotary Natural Science Center, on lakeshore, has exhibits and activities for children and adults. Children's Fairyland, across from Garden Center, has carousel, rides, puppet shows, songs and stories on weekends. Oakland Museum, with ecological, art, and history exhibits covering California, is at Tenth and Oak streets.

# Morcom Amphitheater of Roses

❀ 700 Jean Street, Oakland

This little-known garden tucked away in an urban setting just a block from Grand Avenue is aptly named, for it is in a natural bowl. The seven-and-one-half-acre site, purchased by the city from a private landowner in 1915 and transformed into a rose garden in the early 1930s by the Business Men's Garden Club and the fledgling East Bay Rose Society, was designed as a composite of the Renaissance gardens of Italy. Oakland has celebrated Rose Sunday in the garden every year since 1934; since 1954 this event has coincided with Mother's Day and the city's Mother of the Year program.

Entry is through classical pillars from the open end of the bowl along the main axis of the formal gardens. Oaks, stone pines, buckeyes, and redwoods on the surrounding hillsides emphasize the sense of enclosure. Over 500 varieties of roses, including American Rose Society award winners, are arranged in a series of long beds. Rose bushes surround a central pool and radiate from another circle of roses. In summer the potpourri aroma of thousands of blooms floats on the breeze.

The wide central path has many plaques set in concrete, com-

*Classical touches among fragrant roses*

memorating Oakland's Mothers of the Year. Climbing roses on wrought-iron arches marking four sets of steps opposite each other give a pleasing symmetry to this part of the garden.

A double staircase on the hillside left of the main entrance leads to terraces on three levels. The uppermost and largest has raised flower beds, many benches and tables, and fine views across the garden. Pools empty into a narrow channel cascading between stairs to the lower level. Pink-flowered 'Pride of Oakland' roses make a blooming hedge on either side. The upper terrace is a favorite place for weddings in spring and early summer when the roses are at peak bloom. The show of blossoms continues into fall.

**Getting There:** Highway 580 to Oakland; take Grand Avenue exit east, go to Jean Street, turn left, and go one block. Park on street.

**Admission:** Free. Open daily dawn to dusk.

**Facilities:** Restrooms, drinking fountains, benches, tables. Rose pruning demonstrations in January. Handicapped access generally good, but women's restroom has steep steps. To rent space for events call (415) 273-3186.

**Nearby:** Many shops and restaurants on Grand Avenue; Lakeside Park along Lake Merritt, Oakland-East Bay Garden Center, and Kaiser Center roof garden are a few blocks away.

# Kaiser Center Roof Garden

❀ Harrison and 20th Streets, Oakland

Rooftop landscapes are not uncommon today, but in 1959, when the twenty-three-story Kaiser Center building across from Lake Merritt was constructed, landscape architects Osmundson and Staley were confronted with the unusual challenge of designing a landscape for the three-acre roof of the adjacent parking garage, five floors above the street.

The main problems in constructing any roof garden are drainage and weight. The Kaiser Center garden relies on the drainage system of the concrete roof slab itself, consisting of catch basins and downspouts at alternate columns of the garage structure, with surrounding areas sloping almost imperceptibly to drain individual areas of roof and garden. There is also a four-inch layer of light-weight drain rock beneath the soil, concrete paving, and structures of the landscape, which permits continuous subsurface drainage over the entire roof.

The problem of weight was handled by limiting soil in lawn and groundcover areas to six inches and using a light-weight soil mix to construct the thirty-inch mounds on which trees and shrubs are planted. Large specimen trees, which when planted were as tall as twenty feet and weighed up to three tons, are placed directly over supporting columns, and all rocks and boulders are light-weight pumice stone. Trees with shallow, fibrous root systems were selected so that they would accommodate themselves to the shallow soil.

The park-like garden today has mature cork oaks, magnolias, and olive trees and large swaths of lawn overlooking a shallow pool. The pool can be crossed by a footbridge to a patio where double doors lead to a restaurant and shops. Diners look out on the garden through a wall of windows.

A patio at the north end of the garden, with benches for those who prefer to bring their own lunches, is backed by a long, curved bed of roses. A shady corridor lined with pittosporums shelters mature rhododendrons and azaleas. A landscape plan of the garden, with plants labeled, is centrally located beside the path.

Lake Merritt is a stop on the Pacific flyway for migrating birds, which come swooping in between tall buildings to enjoy this green oasis in the city. Planes and helicopters cross the sky; the lunchtime crowd and the birds acknowledge them, apparently accepting that gardens, too, are not always earth-bound.

**Getting There:** Highway 880 to Oakland; exit at Oak Street and continue to Lake Merritt (Oak Street becomes

*Diners enjoy lush garden beyond wall of glass*

Lakeside Drive). Kaiser Center complex is on left before intersection of Lakeside and Harrison Street. Use metered parking along Lakeside Drive or parking garage behind buildings. From garage take elevator to roof garden (Kaiser Building D level/20th Street Mall).

**Admission:** Open daily 7am to 7pm.

**Facilities:** Benches, drinking fountain, restrooms inside building. Handicapped access good. Shops, restaurant on same level as roof garden. Art exhibits often on display in corridors near elevators and escalator.

**Nearby:** Stroll around Lake Merritt and visit Rotary Science Center, Oakland-East Bay Garden Center, and Children's Fairyland in Lakeside Park. Oakland Museum, at Tenth and Oak streets, has an interesting landscape, partly on roof, and exhibits illustrating natural landscapes of California, as well as native American and Gold Rush artifacts. Museum is noted for collections of art of western America.

# Dunsmuir House

❀ 2960 Peralta Oaks Court, Oakland

The nearly fifty acres of gardens and woods surrounding romantic Dunsmuir House are set like a gem in the midst of summer-dry hills. Built in 1899, this was the summer home of the family of I.W. Hellman, one of the founders of Wells Fargo Bank. In 1971 a citizens group helped to restore the house and grounds, which have been owned and operated by the City of Oakland since 1961.

Following the path from the entry gate, visitors immediately see many of the large specimen trees that give this site distinction, including coast live oaks on the hills and along the creek, Atlas cedars, southern magnolias, black locusts, Japanese yews, and Canary Island date palms. Tall eucalypts, Monterey pines, and oaks shade lawns and house, a frequent setting for garden parties,

*Restored mansion among oak-studded hills*

charity events, flower shows, and an annual Christmas celebration. Visitors may enjoy the areas near the Colonial Revival-style mansion, including an old log cabin and picnic tables beside a pond, or explore further.

Around the sag pond, a reminder of the Hayward earthquake fault, are bamboos, Australian tree ferns, native woodwardia ferns, sedges, rushes, Abyssinian banana, elephant ear, and papyrus, a mixture that complements the lacy white gazebo at water's edge. Ducks and swans are permanent residents here.

The road along the creek and the areas between paths have other outstanding trees — Japanese maples, dogwoods, deodar cedars, blue Atlas cedars, ginkgoes, native big-leaf maples, redwoods, and bay laurels. Trees not often seen in Northern California include hornbeam, incense cedar, Colorado blue spruce, and Mexican palo verde. Many shrubs and seasonal flowers can be enjoyed as one strolls.

Near an old, sway-backed farm shed, chicken coop, dairy barn, and stable is a carriage house, where artifacts and old photographs are displayed and books, gifts, and a guide to plants in the gardens can be purchased. Benches at this end of the garden provide good views of surrounding hills. Tall cottonwood trees along the creek, their leaves rustling in the slightest breeze, turn into a shower of gold in autumn.

Back toward the house is a cactus garden with opuntia cactus, the fruits of which were eaten by native Americans in desert regions. There is also a succulent garden and an enclosed pool, bath house, and grotto, fallen into charming ruin.

**Getting There:** Highway 580 to 106th Avenue exit in south Oakland. Turn toward hills on 106th to Peralta Oaks Drive. Turn right, then left onto Peralta Oaks Court. Park on street or in nearby parking lots.

**Admission:** Donation requested to tour grounds; children free. House tours, adults, $3; seniors and children under 12, $2. Open Sundays only, noon to 4pm April through September. Guided tours of house at 1, 2, and 3pm. Self-guided tours of grounds.

**Facilities:** Benches, picnic tables, drinking fountains, gift shop. Handicapped access excellent. For information about events, call (415) 562-0329. For group tours or to rent facilities, call (415) 562-7588.

**Nearby:** Also in Oakland are Morcom Amphitheater of Roses, Kaiser Center roof garden, and Oakland-East Bay Garden Center.

# Tao House

❀ Danville

Tao House, built for playwright Eugene O'Neill and his wife Carlotta, is a place of withdrawal—walled-in, quiet, with spectacular views of Mt. Diablo, the San Ramon Valley, and the Las Trampas Hills. Fourteen acres and the house are now a national historic site.

Tao means right path or way. O'Neill was not a Taoist, but he spent his life in search of truth, and he was familiar with Chinese philosophy. The O'Neills discovered the 158-acre Danville site when he was recovering from illness, and O'Neill declared it would be "final home and harbor for me." Soon after he was awarded the Nobel Prize in 1936, they bought the property, built Tao House, and developed the area around the house into a well-tended, walled garden.

Gingers, ferns, and mosses nestle among volcanic rocks near the door, and low boxwood hedges define brick walks. Wisteria drapes the front porch as it did when the O'Neills lived there. (There is a photo of O'Neill, clippers in hand, poised to attack overgrown wisteria). A chinaberry tree (*Melia azedarach*), from the original plantings, is struggling after being damaged in a storm, and an enormous oak in front of the house shows signs of being struck by lightning. California sycamores, which grow well in the hot, dry hills, line the circular drive leading to the walled garden.

White-flowered oleanders, wisteria, and campanula (bellflower) echo the brick house, which is painted white, inside and out. Floors and front gate are black, and roof tiles are grayish black, more oriental than Spanish. Colorful touches are the rust-red shutters matching brick porch and walks, purple-leaf plum trees, and old hawthorns with berries and leaves that brighten in autumn.

Brick paths zig-zag behind the house and down to the pool, in deference to the Taoist belief that evil moves only in straight lines. Carlotta wondered in her diary who would benefit from the redwoods they planted to screen the pool. Visitors now enjoy them, as well as the mature pines and oaks. Old almond and walnut trees also remain on the sunny hillside.

The house and garden look out from behind protective walls. It was inward exploration, too, that marked O'Neill's most creative work. The five plays he wrote here include *Long Day's Journey Into Night*, for which he won his fourth Pulitzer Prize. O'Neill did not find final harbor at Tao House, after all, but died on the East Coast, where the O'Neills lived the last decade of his life.

*Young trees soon will shade walled courtyard garden*

**Getting There:** The National Park Service runs two vans daily to Tao House, leaving from clock tower in Danville. Take Highway 680 to Danville; exit at Diablo Road, turn west, and go downtown. At clock tower drive under archway to rear lot and park in long-term spaces.

**Admission:** Free. Open daily all year. Tours Wednesday through Sunday 10am and 1:30pm. Reservations required. Call (415) 838-0249.

**Facilities:** Restrooms, benches, museum, gift shop. Handicapped access limited.

**Nearby:** Restored Old Town in Danville is interesting to explore. Heather Farm Park and Garden Center, with demonstration gardens, is on Marchbanks Drive in Walnut Creek, and conservationist John Muir's house is a short drive north in Martinez.

# John Muir House

❀ 4202 Alhambra Avenue, Martinez

If naturalist and conservationist John Muir today were to go up to the belltower of the house built in 1882 by his wife's parents, and where he and his wife Louie lived for many years, he might be saddened to see that the once agricultural Alhambra Valley is now filled with residential and commercial development. But his view to the south would be much the same as it was when the Muirs lived there — fruit orchards, an adobe house, and the bridge across Franklin Creek over which teams of horses pulled wagonloads of fruit. A restored carriage house and windmill are in their original locations. The nine-acre property is now a national historic site.

Crusader for national parks, founder of the Sierra Club, and influential writer of books such as *The Mountains of California* (1894), *My First Summer in the Sierra* (1911), and *Travels in Alaska* (1915), Muir made a good living from the bounty of these orchards, but left for his beloved mountains whenever he felt certain that his wife and two daughters were well provided for. "Wilderness," he claimed, "is a necessity."

He wrote affectionately of the garden and grounds he planted with the help of his wife and father-in-law. Incense cedars, a tree

*America's most celebrated naturalist*

much admired by Muir and possibly brought from the mountains, tall palms beside the front porch, a California bay laurel by the driveway, and a giant sequoia planted about 1890 survive from earlier times. Old roses and many flowers are planted as they were when Mrs. Muir won prizes for flower arrangements.

Bartlett pears and grapes were the most important cash crops, but peaches, cherries, almonds, apples, walnuts, and citrus also were cultivated. Pomegranates and olives were grown for family use. An herb garden has been recreated by the Muir Garden Club.

Native buckeyes, oaks, and elderberries grow along the road by the creek, and a small garden of native plants, including sages, manzanitas, gooseberries, Pacific Coast irises, and poppies, is under development. It is a short walk past small orchards to the adobe house where Muir's daughter and her husband lived and where Muir played with his grandchildren. An arbor shades picnic tables behind this house.

In spite of prosperity, Muir was restless. He wrote that he was "busy thinning apricots and peaches . . . how little of my real work I accomplish in the midst of all this ranch work! . . . How grand would be a home in a hollow sequoia!"

**Getting There:** Highway 680 or 80 to Highway 4 (John Muir Parkway/Franklin Canyon Road) exit near Martinez. Follow signs and turn on Alhambra Avenue. Park in lot.

**Admission:** Adults, $1; children under 17, free. House and grounds open daily 10am to 4:30pm except major holidays. Group tours by reservation. Call (415) 228-8860.

**Facilities:** Restrooms, drinking fountain, picnic tables, benches. Handicapped access good on site; call in advance for transportation up hill to house. Guide book, with map, and brochures and books about and by Muir available at entrance. Film about Muir shown hourly. Sierra Club exhibit room. Annual celebration of Muir's birthday in April.

**Nearby:** The village of Port Costa was a bustling center of grain export from the Central Valley at the turn of the century. Across the Sacramento River is the historic town of Benicia, an early contender for the capital of California with restored capitol building and old garden, as well as other original homes and churches. Mt. Diablo, with magnificent views on clear days, and Eugene O'Neill's house and garden are to the south in Danville.

# Also of Interest

**Ardenwood Farm Regional Preserve**, 34600 Ardenwood Boulevard, Fremont (415) 796-0663. Restored century-old house, working farm using old techniques, old apple varieties in orchard, kitchen gardens; two-acre landscape around house with old roses, fine trees and shrubs.

**Berkeley Horticultural Nursery**, 1310 McGee Avenue, Berkeley (415) 526-4704. City block of unusual plants, including natives; many hard-to-find bulbs in fall; small garden of permanent plantings; specialty plant catalogs.

**Heather Farm Park and Garden Center**, 1540 Marchbanks Drive, Walnut Creek (415) 947-1678. Five acres under development as demonstration gardens keyed to local climate; native plants, sensory garden, children's adventure gardens, water-conserving landscape; classes, workshops, plant sales and shows.

**Magic Gardens Nursery**, 729 Heinz Avenue, Berkeley (415) 644-1992. Full-service nursery and landscape design service; high-quality native and exotic plants for temperate Pacific region; fine catalog also gives notice of plant and flower shows and information on cultivation practices.

# San Jose/South Bay

# 3.

# Hakone Japanese Garden

❀ 21000 Big Basin Way, Saratoga

The serenity of this garden in the hills of Saratoga seems centuries removed from the bustle of nearby Silicon Valley. Hakone was once the vacation retreat of wealthy San Franciscans Oliver and Isabel Stine, for whom the garden was designed and constructed in 1918. Striving for authenticity, Mrs. Stine retained a Japanese architect, Tsunematsu Shintani, and one of the emperor's former gardeners, Naoharu Aihara, to create a hill-and-water garden typical of seventeenth-century Japan. Because of the design, attention to detail, and use of Japanese garden art, Hakone is considered by many to be the only authentic Japanese garden in the United States. The property has been a Saratoga city park since 1966.

The garden consists of three levels. On the lowest level is the "heart" of the garden — the pond — where koi fish, symbols of longevity because they live many decades, swim lazily among water-lilies. An island here in the shape of a turtle is another symbol of longevity. On the middle level of the garden is a "moon-viewing hill" and a house built without nails in the style favored by traditional Japanese cabinet-makers. Also on the middle level is the Master Stone, the anchor to which the three-level design is related. This

*Trees and shrubs pruned to maintain balanced composition*

stone is placed in the spot most conducive to appreciating the entire garden as a symbol of the harmony of heaven, earth, and man. The highest point of the garden — symbolically the "mountain" — represents harmony between sky and earth.

As are most Japanese gardens, for much of the year Hakone is a study in greens, grays, and browns, deriving its beauty and interest primarily from form, texture, and composition. But as early as January the garden lights up with the colorful flowers of hundreds of azaleas and camellias. Flowering cherries and wisteria come later in spring. A special treat is the fine collection of bamboos grown from cuttings and seeds by members of the Japanese Bamboo Society of Saratoga. Japanese maples and cypresses were imported as mature plants from Japan when the garden was taking shape. The largest cypresses are now estimated to be 300 to 500 years old.

**Getting There:** Highway 880 or 280 to downtown Saratoga. Go west on Highway 9 (Big Basin Way) less than a mile. Watch for sign on left. Up long driveway, park in lot outside gates.

**Admission:** Donation requested. Open Monday through Friday 10am to 5pm, Saturdays and Sundays 11am to 5pm. Closed legal holidays.

**Facilities:** Restrooms. Brochure. Handicapped access limited, but views can be enjoyed from lower level. Children under 10 must be accompanied by adult. No food, drinks, pets, radios, or musical instruments allowed in garden. Picnic tables outside gates. For information call (408) 867-3438.

**Nearby:** Enjoy lunch and shopping in the village of Saratoga, or continue up Highway 9 about three miles to Congress Springs Winery.

# Villa Montalvo

❀ 15400 Montalvo Road, Saratoga

The country home of James D. Phelan, son of Gold Rush pioneers, is set in the wooded hills of Saratoga. Phelan inherited, then added to, his father's wealth from San Francisco real estate and banking. As did his father, he participated in business, political, and cultural affairs, and he served as California senator from 1915 to 1921. His travels in Europe inspired him to create a retreat for artists and writers patterned on similar centers in Europe. In 1912 he built his dream house, Villa Montalvo, to showcase his love for culture and the arts.

Only five acres around Villa Montalvo are cultivated. The rest of the land, with hiking trails and visitors center, is managed by the Santa Clara County Parks and Recreation Department. Phelan's will directed that the house and gardens be used for the development of literature, music, and the arts; today artists live and work in residence here, and many exhibits, plays, and musical events are held outdoors in the warmer months of the year.

From the north-portico terrace of the knoll-top mansion, which is draped with white and purple wisteria, views sweep down across lawns to a columned gazebo. Phelan admired Roman antiquities, and statuary is placed in niches and bowers here and elsewhere in the garden. Stone benches, marble figures, and a large urn with fountain overlook a woodland of pines and eucalypts. The cypress-lined path, with clipped boxwood hedges, features a circular bed with an unusual shrub, bird nest cypress (*Chamaecyparis lawsoniana* 'Nidiformis'). In this area also, among other fruit trees, is a pawpaw tree (*Asimina triloba*), seldom grown in California but native to the eastern and southeastern United States. It has long, drooping leaves, large purple flowers, and edible fruit.

Guests came from many places to enjoy Phelan's hospitality. They must have admired the tall cypresses, magnolias, bunya-bunya trees (*Araucaria bidwillii*), birches, and valley oaks. Beds of annuals and shrubs, variegated English holly, sweet olive, bush germander, and an English laurel hedge border the lawn.

An Egyptian area near the house has an obelisk, sphinxes, and a griffin-legged bench, said to have been brought from Egypt by Phelan. Camperdown elms close by were planted in 1913 when the gardens were begun, as were the forsythia behind the bench, creeping St. Johnswort, horsechestnut trees, santolina, and swarms of daffodils along a wooded path leading to a small white gazebo.

A Spanish courtyard on the south side of the house is the heart of Montalvo. The sunny, brick-floored court with arched

*Pendulous branches of weeping cherry are attractive out of leaf*

loggias, palms, and plants in terra cotta pots has a circular fountain and luxuriant wisteria draped on balconies.

A former swimming pool has been filled in and planted with grass. There is also an 800-seat amphitheater, where guests once lounged on cushions and blankets to listen to poetry readings, dramas, and recitals.

Many celebrities, artists, and writers enjoyed the hospitality of Senator Phelan at Villa Montalvo. Visitors still delight in this beautiful setting, and the arts still flourish as Phelan wished.

**Getting There:** Highway 880 in Los Gatos to Highway 9 (Saratoga Avenue) exit toward Saratoga. Go about 3.5 miles, turn left on Montalvo Road, and continue through residential area to entry. Park in lots 2, 3, or 4 and follow signs.

**Admission:** Donation requested. Open weekdays 8am to 5pm; weekends 9am to 5pm. Gallery open Thursdays and Fridays 1 to 4pm, Saturdays and Sundays 11am to 4pm.

**Facilities:** Restrooms at parking lot 4, benches, hiking trails, gift shop, nature displays, books, maps, and information at visitors center. No picnicking in park. Art exhibits, plays, musical events in spring and summer; annual Garden Theatre Gala; fund-raising yuletide show and sale. For group tours or to inquire about events, call (408) 741-3421. For information on hiking trails and nature area call (408) 867-0190.

**Nearby:** Carman's Nursery, offering rare and unusual perennials, rock garden plants, and bonsai starters, is on East Mozart Avenue in Los Gatos.

# Saso Herb Gardens

❀ 14625 Fruitvale Avenue, Saratoga

An early 1900s refurbished farmhouse and barn are surrounded by fragrant herbs, and a spectacular old live oak tree spreads above the house and patio. Here, just a few blocks from Saratoga's city hall, Louis and Virginia Saso share the fascinating world of herbs not only through their nursery but with classes, workshops, and guided walks. Herbs, as they say, have been used for centuries; to grow herbs for food and medicine is to discover an old wisdom.

In this beautiful setting the Sasos grow over 1,000 herbs — about sixty kinds of sage, for instance, and fifteen to twenty kinds of oregano. Many culinary, medicinal, and ornamental herbs are for sale, as are scented geraniums, dried wreaths, swags, and bouquets. But the primary goals are to educate others about the

*Saint Fiacre presides over aromatic herbs*

benefits of herbs and to promote organic gardening methods.

An astrological garden radiates from a circle in the center of which is a wood figure of Saint Fiacre, the seventh-century saint of gardeners. Each of twelve beds features herbs said to relate to a particular sign in the zodiac.

Medicinal herbs favored by native Americans are planted as an Indian medicine wheel. Horehound, wild licorice, and sage are just a few of the plants used. A biblical garden has lilies, crown-of-thorns, St. Johnswort, passion vine, and other plants with biblical references.

Plants are grown in a mixture of potting soil and nutrient-rich material composted on the premises. No chemical sprays or fertilizers are used. In keeping with organic methods of insect control, garlic chives have been planted as companion plants around a bed of miniature roses. An old rose on the fence is grown for its large hips, rich in vitamin C.

Redwoods, a tall Atlas cedar, fig, lemon, and other fruit trees are interspersed among the herb beds. But the tree that excites Louis is his neem tree (*Azadirachta indica*), native to India. Called the tree of paradise, it could be a valuable plant for impoverished lands, he says, because every part is useful.

**Getting There:** Highway 880 in Los Gatos to Highway 9 (Saratoga Avenue) exit toward Saratoga. Turn right on Fruitvale Avenue and continue to corner of Farwell. Park near entry gate.

**Admission:** Free. Open Monday through Saturday 9am to 2:30pm or by appointment.

**Facilities:** Restrooms, benches. Handicapped access limited. Brochures, booklets, plants, dried materials. Guided tours. Spring and summer open house. Harvest fair. Speakers and workshops (reservations required). Call (408) 867-0307.

**Nearby:** Villa Montalvo is nearby on Montalvo Road, and Hakone Japanese Garden is on Big Basin Way. Take Highway 9 up past Hakone to Big Basin Redwoods State Park, the first state redwood park (established 1902), with miles of hiking trails and natural history museum.

# San Jose Rose Garden

❀ Naglee Avenue, San Jose

Imagine the fragrance and color of 7,500 rose bushes of 150 varieties on five and one-half acres and you will have some idea of the magnificence of this San Jose showplace.

Inspired by the Santa Clara County Rose Society, and through its efforts, the municipal rose garden was begun in 1931. Peak bloom is in May, but there are so many different kinds of roses — old roses, modern hybrids, miniatures, bush roses, tree roses, climbers — that for many months something is always in flower.

From the wrought-iron main entrance gates a path leads to a turquoise-blue fountain and circular reflecting pool. Plants are labeled, and wide asphalt paths make it easy for visitors of all ages and levels of mobility to enjoy the garden. Benches are shaded by groups of cotoneasters and pyracanthas pruned to reveal twisted trunks. Rose beds are arranged in symmetrical patterns. Some plants are grouped by flower color, so there are swaths of yellow, red, white, peach, silvery gray, and pink.

A rock-walled terrace with tall redwood trees on a knoll behind it is a favorite place for graduation and wedding ceremonies. At such times, grass playfields of the adjacent park are set with chairs, and the sweet aroma of roses permeates the air.

**Getting There:** Highway 880 (Highway 17) in San Jose to North Bascom Avenue exit; continue east to Naglee Avenue and turn left. Park on street.

**Admission:** Free. Open daily 8am to sunset.

**Facilities:** Restrooms, benches, picnic tables, drinking fountains, playfields. Handicapped access excellent. No dogs except guides-to-the-blind. Brochure with map and names of roses available from gardeners on duty. To arrange tours or events call (408) 277-4000.

**Nearby:** Also on Naglee Avenue is Rosicrucian Park, with Egyptian museum and art gallery. Overfelt Gardens is on Educational Park Drive, and Kelley Park Japanese Friendship Garden is on Senter Road. Winchester Mystery House, with shops and restaurants across street, is on Winchester Boulevard between Stevens Creek Boulevard and Highway 280.

# Rosicrucian Park

❀ 1342 Naglee Avenue, San Jose

The architecture suggests Thebes, Karnak, temples on the Nile, but it's Rosicrucian Park, a complex of gardens, courtyards, and buildings set in a residential neighborhood. The Egyptian museum here houses the largest collection of Egyptian, Babylonian, and Assyrian antiquities in the western United States. Headquarters for the worldwide fraternity of the Rosicrucian Order, the complex also contains a planetarium, auditorium, research library, administrative offices, and facilities of the Rose-Croix University.

Wide lawns, tall palm trees creating shadow patterns against walls, deeply recessed entrances to inner courtyards, a colossal obelisk, and gate portals incised with Egyptian writing add to the exotic feeling of this unusual park. The main entrance pylons at

*Fan palms mimic rounded dome and columns of astronomy building*

Naglee and Park avenues are reproductions of temple portals at Medinet Habu, Egypt. A curving walk, accented by oleanders, leads to the obelisk, flanked by a pair of large, gray sphinxes representing the sun-god Horus, then back to a courtyard with an impressive statue of Augustus Caesar. Benches shaded by pollarded sycamore trees and palms look across to a sunken court where a golden figure with outstretched arms reflects the sun. A mosaic of Akhnaton in a chariot covers the wall of one of the buildings. The statues, obelisk, and other art works in the park commemorate figures important in ancient Egyptian history and religion or in the development of the Rosicrucian philosophy.

Tall columns mark the entrance to the museum and art gallery, a stately building with wide steps, reclining ram statues, and lofty palms on either side. A statue of a standing hippopotamus, representing the deity Taurt, rises from a pool centered in the walk. Behind the museum a Camperdown elm spreads umbrella-like above benches. Many palms, a bunya-bunya tree, redwoods, beds of flowers, and chimes ringing in the breeze make this court ideal for contemplation or quiet conversation.

Around the corner on Randol Avenue is a double walkway to the research library, with a double row of palms and a center divider filled with feathery papyrus about ten feet tall. Fibers from this grass-like perennial were used in ancient times to make parchment. A wide lawn is dotted with birch trees and five rows of tree roses. Opposite is a large mayten and a dawn redwood tree. Lights above the library doors are patterned after lotus blossoms.

There is a restful area across from the parking lot on Chapman Avenue with large trees, reflecting pool, benches, a walk with boxwood hedges on each side, and welcome shade on summer days from huge black walnut trees and magnolias. Roses and yews accent the pool. A breezeway between buildings leads to comfortable tables and chairs under a fruitless mulberry tree. Hanging baskets of flowers attract hummingbirds.

**Getting There:** Highway 880 (Highway 17) in San Jose to North Bascom Avenue exit east to Naglee Avenue. Turn left, go to Chapman Street, and turn right. Park in lot or on street.

**Admission:** Garden free, open daily. Museum and art gallery: adults, $3; seniors $2.50; ages 12-17, $1; under 12, free; open 9am to 5pm Tuesday through Sunday. Planetarium: adults, $2; seniors, $1.50; under 18, $1; under 7, free; open weekdays 1 to 4:30pm with shows at 2pm, and weekends noon to 4:30pm with shows at 2 and 3:30pm.

**Facilities:** Restrooms, drinking fountains, benches. No picnicking. Handicapped access excellent on grounds. Brochures, books, and gifts at museum. Continuous exhibits in art gallery. For information call (408) 287-9171.

# Overfelt Gardens

❀ Educational Park Drive, San Jose

A few blocks from two busy freeways, Overfelt Gardens, a city park of thirty-three acres, is a place of peace and solitude, as the donor wished. It is a park for walking, enjoying birds and small wildlife, and watching seasonal changes.

Mildred Overfelt, daughter of early pioneers who came to San Jose in the 1850s, donated the land, part of the family's 160-acre homestead. Before it was moved, the old Overfelt house was shaded by the largest oak tree in the park.

Since its opening in 1966, development of the garden has followed Miss Overfelt's plan for a restful park with planted sections as well as natural areas for wildlife sanctuary. Two lakes, seen from the deck at the entrance kiosk, attract migratory water birds and also serve as percolation ponds to help maintain Santa Clara Valley aquifers. Buckeyes, sycamores, oaks, grasses, and native wildflowers grow around the lakes.

There is a fine collection of palms, including seven varieties of fan and feather palms. Benches beneath them, and across the lawn, offer good views. Paths from here lead past valley, cork, holly, and coast live oaks. Other trees are magnolias, liquidambar, ginkgo

*Mixed grove of palms displays varied shapes and sizes*

(lovely in autumn), bay laurel, and several kinds of pines. Jelecote pine from Mexico, up to eighty feet tall, is notable for its soft, drooping needles. A fragrance garden, iris beds, roses, and a fountain in memory of Miss Overfelt enhance this area.

A small brook winds beside a redwood-shaded path to the Chinese Cultural Center, a five-acre garden with cottonwood trees, benches, and a fifteen-foot bronze statue of Confucius on a marble base, reflected in a tranquil pond. This area is landscaped with flowering crabapples, purple-leaf plums, birches, and native oak trees. A five-sided pavilion is symbolic of the five-petaled plum blossom. The Friendship Gate is a gift from the people of Taiwan.

Beside steps rising up to the beautifully detailed Sun Yat Sen Memorial Hall are beds of fragrant jasmine with holly, ginkgo, and Chinese flame trees. From the steps there is a fine view across the lake. Flowering quinces, cherries, jasmine, and magnolias at each corner frame the Chiang Kai-shek Pavilion.

Shrubs along the paths include pyracantha and cotoneaster with colorful fall berries that attract birds. Oaks, willows, cattails, and native plants are at the water's edge. Benches are placed to give good views of the natural and constructed beauty of the gardens.

**Getting There:** Highway 101 in San Jose to McKee Road exit east; go to Educational Park Drive and turn left. Park in lot.

**Admission:** Free. Open daily 10am to sunset.

**Facilities:** Restrooms, benches, picnic tables, drinking fountains. Handicapped access excellent. Guide to arboreal trail, brochure about gardens, and information about Chinese Cultural Center available at entrance kiosk. Park rangers answer questions and lead tour groups. To arrange tours call (408) 251-3323 or 259-5477. No bicycles, skate boards, dogs, sports, or water activities allowed in park. Relief model of Overfelt Gardens, showing existing and planned development, displayed at San Jose Public Library adjacent to park.

**Nearby:** Buddhist Temple Japanese Garden is on North Fifth Street. Prusch Farm Park, with historic house and community gardens, is on South King Road. Symons Nursery and Antiques is on Willow Street.

# Kelley Park Japanese Garden

❀ 1300 Senter Road, San Jose

At the approximate mid-point of the city's Coyote Creek Park corridor, a few blocks from the Santa Clara County Fairgrounds, is San Jose's popular Kelley Park, a 176-acre recreational area with picnic sites, zoo, carousel, reception and conference center, and historical museum. Of special interest to garden enthusiasts is the Japanese Friendship Garden, patterned after the Korakuen Garden in Okayama, Japan, sister city to San Jose, and a joint project of that Japanese city and Pacific Neighbors, a San Jose community group.

The Japanese garden, on about six and one-half acres, is dominated by three lakes whose surrounding landscapes differ yet are harmonious. An arched bridge on the upper lake, a fine place to watch koi fish, leads to islands where pruned pines, azaleas, and pittosporums seem to embrace large rocks. Onshore, among beech, pine, and birch trees, a bench on a high bank overlooks the lake, and from paths around the lake the water is in constant view.

Downhill toward the middle lake, red railings line a walk among blue Atlas cedars and mounds planted with low-pruned pines and azaleas. A small waterfall tumbles into a stream that flows to the lake. Flowering cherries are a special attraction in spring bloom, and tall cedars, lace-leaf maples, pruned hollies, and rhododendrons create a feeling of seclusion here. Ornamental grasses at one end of the lake rustle in the slightest breeze.

A bridge crosses a neck of the middle lake. Further on, flat rocks zig-zag among waterlilies and irises to a teahouse, where, among clumps of bamboo and crape myrtles blooming in white puffs, tables and chairs are placed for taking light refreshments on a deck overlooking the water. Refreshments also are served inside the teahouse, where Japanese art and books are displayed. Native oaks and redwoods grow near a ceremonial basin and a gate leading to other parts of Kelley Park.

A path rises to the third lake, where a five-story pagoda is prominently placed on a high point. A curved concrete bridge spans the stream above. Enormous southern magnolias and two ancient olive trees, pruned into mounds, break up a rolling expanse of lawn. Curving beds of white daisies, pomegranates, pink crape myrtle, barberry, prostrate cotoneaster, purple-leaf plums, and maples contrast pleasantly with the green background of pines and other evergreen trees. Stone lanterns of varied design are placed at symbolic locations in close harmony with plants.

Feathery sago palms, native to Japan, lend an airy feeling to

*Rocks, water, and low, spreading pines are favored in Japanese gardens*

the entrance gate. The Friendship Gate, constructed in 1987, was completed with funds raised by Pacific Neighbors and San Jose's Japanese-American community. Dedication of the gate brought new awareness of this magnificent thirty-year-old garden.

**Getting There:** Highway 101 south in San Jose to Story Road exit west to Senter Road. Turn left to Kelley Park. Park in lot.

**Admission:** Free, but $2 parking. Open daily 10am to sundown. Teahouse open Wednesday through Friday 11am to 2:30pm; Saturday and Sunday 11am to 4pm; closed December through February. For group reservations, call (408) 277-4193.

**Facilities:** Restrooms, drinking fountains, benches, picnic tables. Handicapped access good.

**Nearby:** The adjacent San Jose Historical Museum has early San Jose buildings with furnishings and historic artifacts. Living History Days in May recreate Santa Clara Valley life a century ago. Victorian Christmas celebrates the holidays with special events. For information or to rent meeting rooms call (408) 287-2290. Museum hours: 10am to 4:30pm Monday through Friday; noon to 4:30pm Saturday and Sunday. Happy Hollow Children's Park and Baby Zoo open daily except Christmas: Monday through Saturday 10am to 5pm; Sunday 11am to 6pm. For information call (408) 295-8383.

# Hecker Pass Family Adventure

❀ 3050 Hecker Pass Road, Gilroy

West of Gilroy, the Santa Clara Valley town known for its garlic production and festival, a new theme park is taking shape. The park and its lush gardens are the dream of Michael Bonfante, president of Nob Hill Foods, a central California grocery chain.

Bonfante, also owner of wholesale Tree Haven Nursery, which specializes in large, container-grown trees, is a long-time nature lover. The eighty-acre Hecker Pass site, with forty acres in park and forty more in support services, is under construction in 1989.

Discovery Park Lake has three waterfalls, huge boulders, observation decks overhanging the water, and stone walks and walls that follow the lakeshore. Ducks and other water birds already are making their homes around the recently constructed lake. A two-acre landscape with lush lawns, flower beds filled with a changing display, native trees (sycamore, oak, pine, willow, redwood), shrubs, and ground covers, received the 1987 California Landscape Contractors Sweepstakes Trophy as the best new California landscape. The finished gardens will have over 500 kinds of native plants, placed to enhance the natural beauty of the site.

Several separate plantings will be based on four California geographic zones, from the Sierra to the desert, from the Central Valley to the south coast. Another special area will be an Enchanted Forest, with trees (mostly sycamores) grafted, pruned, split, bound, and twisted into braids, circles, diamonds, hearts, and ladder shapes.

Train rides around the park, children's petting zoo, habitat for native California animals and birds, restaurant, picnic and barbecue areas, paddle and sail boats on the lake, amphitheater for outdoor events, model western town, and stagecoach and pony rides are some of the attractions planned.

**Getting There:** Highway 101 south of San Jose to Gilroy; take Highway 152 (Hecker Pass Road) west to park.

**Admission:** Proposed opening summer 1990. Call (408) 842-2121 for information.

**Nearby:** At the top of the pass are the redwood forests of Mt. Madonna park, with small wineries dotting surrounding hills. Goldsmith Seeds, with fields of flowers in bloom in summer, is also on Hecker Pass Road. Continue west to Roses of Yesterday and Today, in Watsonville, then down Highway 1 to Monterey and Carmel.

# Also of Interest

**Buddhist Temple Japanese Garden**, 640 North Fifth Street, San Jose (408) 293-9292. Small garden symbolic of river, lake, and sea; pines, azaleas, statue of Shinren Shonin under large magnolia; temple (built 1863); annex building was temporary shelter for Japanese-Americans returning from internment after World War II.

**Carman's Nursery**, 16201 East Mozart Avenue, Los Gatos (408) 356-0119. Many rare and unusual perennials, rock garden plants, and bonsai starters.

**Goldsmith Seeds**, 2280 Hecker Pass Road, Gilroy (408) 847-7333. Spectacular beds of flowers, new and old varieties in test fields, in bloom June through August.

*Tranquil scene in Buddhist Temple Garden*

**Prusch Farm Park**, 647 South King Road, San Jose (408) 926-5555. Forty-seven acres of Emma Prusch's 1800s dairy farm, now a community park. Community vegetable gardens, historic house, rare-fruit orchard, antique farm implements.

**Symons Nursery & Antiques**, 750 Willow Street, San Jose (408) 295-1875. Full-service, 4.5-acre nursery. Wide selection of trees, roses, many large containers, bird baths, statuary, gift shop, restaurant in antique and country store.

**Winchester Mystery House**, Winchester Boulevard at intersection with Highway 280, San Jose (408) 247-2101. Historic house, landscape with some unusual plants, many old trees, specimen palms; must pay fee for house tour to see gardens.

# Santa Cruz/Monterey

# 4.

# Camp Joy Organic Garden

❀ 131 Camp Joy Road, Boulder Creek

North of Santa Cruz, at a bend in the San Lorenzo River, is a sunny, six-acre meadow surrounded by redwoods, with one and a half acres made into gardens. The property, now known as Camp Joy, was organic gardener Cressie Digby's gift to Jim Nelson, a student of Alan Chadwick, in 1970.

Chadwick, an English horticulturist, brought biodynamic French intensive gardening to America. The system involves growing plants close together in raised beds so that more produce than usual is grown on a piece of land, using much less water. Soil is cultivated by hand, and large amounts of organic compost are incorporated in the garden beds. Underlying the method lies a belief in the earth as a living entity. Chadwick gained fame nationwide through the establishment of a student garden project using this method and teaching classes at the University of California, Santa Cruz.

Camp Joy was begun on a small budget, using cooperative labor to construct a large house, lath house, and greenhouses built from recycled materials. The intent was to create a community-based farm to produce fruit, flowers, vegetables, and herbs while bringing people together and increasing awareness of the need to enrich the land and keep the earth healthy.

A great variety of vegetables is rotated throughout the seasons, and a charming mix of flowers is interplanted among the vegetables, fruit trees, and grape arbors. White and purple Concord grapes are grown for eating and for juice, which is a favorite buy at local health food stores.

Diagonal paths radiate from rose arbors where sweet brier or eglantine (*Rosa eglanteria*) roses are mixed with 'Climbing Cécile Brunner' and 'Mme Alfred Carrière', a Chadwick favorite. Fragrant 'Buff Beauty', a hybrid musk, covers the central gazebo. Petals are saved to make potpourri. Cut roses, penstemons, Michaelmas daisies, dahlias, stock, and a multitude of other flowers are grown for sale, fresh and dried, and to provide bouquets for weddings and other occasions.

Some little-known apples, including 'Fireside', 'Aiken' (a Russian variety), and 'Anoka', are being tried. 'Anoka', obtained from a Bay Area backyard garden, has been very successful. Other vegetable and flower seeds have been donated; a prolific cherry tomato came from seeds contributed by a local resident.

Hives are maintained to provide bees for pollinating plants, and beeswax candles and honey are marketed. Goats and chickens are kept for use by the cooperative household. Several day students and helpers come regularly to learn organic methods.

Camp Joy's primary task is education in intensive, organic food growing, and Camp Joy gardeners reach out to the community to spread these ideas, especially to children. They've been doing it for eighteen years, so they must be onto something.

**Getting There:** From Santa Cruz take Highway 9 north toward Boulder Creek about 12.5 miles. Turn right on Irwin Way, the first right past Brookdale, and follow Irwin across the river. Watch for Tinker's Trail sign on right; shortly, on left, is the Camp Joy sign. Turn left and park by first gate on left.

**Admission:** Donation requested. Visitors stop by informally, but appointments are preferred. Call (408) 338-3651.

**Facilities:** Benches, restrooms. Handicapped access generally good, but paths are bark and dirt. Garden tours, except in winter, for adults and children. Group tours can be arranged. Children's summer classes; apprenticeships; day student and helpers' work offered. Pot lucks; forums on composting and pest management; May basket workshops; plant sale in May; early summer fruit preserving in June; annual wreath sale and open house in November; holiday wreath classes and children's crafts in December. For information call (408) 338-3651.

# U.C. Santa Cruz Arboretum

❀ Empire Grade Road, Santa Cruz

To see rare and unusual plants from New Zealand, Australia, and South Africa, as well as many California natives, visit the University of California, Santa Cruz, Arboretum. The Australian and South African collections here are considered among the best in the world.

The arboretum was begun in 1964 with a gift of ninety species of eucalyptus. There are now some 6,000 kinds of plants from all over the world on fifty acres of the 150-acre site. Plants from the southern hemisphere grow especially well in the mild climate around Monterey Bay. While peak bloom for most plants is in April and May, many flower as early as November and December.

In the fragrant entrance garden a sunny slope is planted with salvias, scented geraniums, lavenders, thymes, and other herbs. Nearby a terraced knoll features succulents and cacti, many contributed by private collectors. The upper terrace overlooks native alders, oaks, willows, and maples and across greenhouse domes. To the west is a breathtaking view of the ocean.

A sloping walk leads down to an amphitheater used for classes and demonstrations. It is nestled beside a stone wall from an old dam, incorporated into the landscape design.

The arboretum has more than 150 varieties of grevillea, drought-tolerant shrubs and trees from Australia with fine-textured foliage, the most common of which, in California landscapes, is the shrubby *Grevillea* 'Noellii'. Woolly grevillea (*G. lanigera*), with red and cream flowers, is attractive to hummingbirds. Shrub-sized *Grevillea* 'Robyn Gordon', with huge red flowers, is a good garden plant.

In addition to eucalypts, the Australian area features yellow-flowered acacias ranging from trees to ground covers. Bottlebrushes are represented by several varieties, and there are many banksias, Australian natives with cones resembling scrub brushes or corn cobs.

In the South African garden are many heaths; *Erica bauera*, with clusters of soft pink or white tubular flowers, is outstanding. The arboretum is well known for its African leucadendrons, leucospermums, and proteas. With proteas, which are reputed to be difficult to grow, the staff says success hinges on benign neglect. *Protea neriifolia* 'Pink Mink', with enormous blooms, its bracts tipped in mink-like fur, is one of the showiest. Protea flowers are popular, and the arboretum has introduced new varieties to the nursery trade.

*Peeling eucalyptus bark strips away to expose smooth trunk*

There is a cypress and podocarp area, and in the New Zealand section are several species of celery pine (*Phyllocladus*), coniferous timber trees with flattened branchlets and leaves reduced to scales. The highest point of this section has good views over the arboretum.

A redwood grove and a pine section are on the perimeter. The canyon garden, viewed from its rim, has large empress trees, with showy purple flowers in mid-spring.

California natives are grown in raised beds beside the parking lot. Manzanitas, lupines, irises, poppies, penstemons, monkeyflowers, coast silktassel, flannel bush, and currants are some featured plants.

**Getting There:** Highway 17 or Highway 1 to Santa Cruz; turn uphill on Bay Street to university campus. At High Street turn left and follow Empire Grade Road to arboretum. Park in lot.

**Admission:** Donation requested. Open Wednesdays, Saturdays, and Sundays 2 to 4pm.

**Facilities:** Restrooms, benches, picnic area, gift shop, map, some plants for sale. Handicapped access good. Docents on site; group tours can be arranged. Spring festival with talks and plant sale third Saturday in May; fall plant sale second Saturday in October. Call (408) 427-2998.

**Nearby:** University of California, Santa Cruz, Farm and Garden are at Bay and High streets.

# U.C. Santa Cruz Farm and Garden

❀ Bay and High Streets, Santa Cruz

At the University of California, Santa Cruz, a four-acre garden on an upper slope of the campus and a twenty-five-acre farm in a lower meadow are operated by the university's agroecology program, which focuses on the development of ecologically, socially, and economically sustainable agricultural systems. In the garden, which was established by Alan Chadwick in 1967, ornamentals, food crops, and native plants are grown using the "biodynamic-French intensive" methods Chadwick introduced to this country, including close spacing of plants in raised beds, maximum soil aeration and drainage, and the use of organic fertilizers. The farm, founded in 1972 and used as a research and teaching facility, includes raised-bed gardens, row crops, orchards, and test plots.

Practices such as companion planting (tomatoes and basil next to each other, for example — said to enhance the flavor of both) and intercropping (such as planting beans, which enrich the soil with nitrogen, along with corn, which protects the beans from beetles) are integral to the program. Many kinds of herbs, perennial and annual flowering plants, vegetables, and fruits are grown organically. Life multiplies life: flowers attract bees that pollinate

*Old redwood barn is still in use*

plants and trees; birds and beneficial insects help control pests. Compost piles are kept from drying wind and sun by a row of locust trees, the leaves of which drop in autumn to become part of the compost. Bordering the garden beds simple wood arbors with roses, jasmine, and other vines are a charming and fragrant accent. On clear days there are beautiful views of Monterey Bay.

Public education is considered important. Through publications, workshops, and conferences, the agroecology program strives to increase awareness about agricultural issues. Results of research and ongoing trials of row crops, fruit trees, and grape vines are shared with the local community.

**Getting There:** Highway 17 or Highway 1 to Santa Cruz; take University of California exit. Turn uphill on Bay Street and go to main campus entrance. Through entrance, follow Coolidge Drive, then take first right turn into parking lot.

**Admission:** Free. Open daily. Offices open weekdays 8am to 5pm.

**Facilities:** Handicapped access very limited. Self-guided tour map of farm at entry gate. Sales of farm and garden products. Call (408) 429-4140.

**Nearby:** University of California, Santa Cruz, Arboretum is on Empire Grade Road. North and east of Santa Cruz are wineries of the Santa Clara Valley. Big Basin Redwoods State Park, the first state redwood park, is off Highway 236, which joins Highway 9 between Santa Cruz and Saratoga; it has miles of hiking trails and a natural history museum.

# Antonelli Brothers Begonias

❀ 2545 Capitola Road, Santa Cruz

Less than two hours south of San Francisco, where filtered sunshine and cooling breezes off Monterey Bay create ideal growing conditions for begonias, is Antonelli Brothers Begonia Gardens, a popular nursery specializing in these colorful plants.

From July through September, when tuberous begonias are in peak bloom, the colors are so intense that they seem to vibrate. Red and orange flower colors are deeply saturated; pink, yellow, apricot, and salmon shades are brilliantly clear; white blooms are pure, shading into rich cream.

In operation since 1935, Antonelli Brothers is a favorite destination for tourists, garden groups, and photographers, who crowd the wide aisles day after day. High ceilings in the barn-like buildings allow the hanging of hundreds of baskets of begonias so that visitors can enjoy the dazzling display from below.

Choosing cascading begonias in hanging baskets or upright varieties for containers or outdoor beds is simplified by a helpful and knowledgeable staff, who joke, during the busy season, that the nursery is open eight days a week. Pacific strain tuberous begonias, which have rose- or carnation-like flowers, are the specialty here. Varieties developed after years of selection and hybridizing include a rose-form type, called the Begonia of Distinction; its blossoms, in a variety of colors, resemble large roses on vigorous, strong stems. Giant ruffled (double and single) begonias are like carnations and camellias; and rose-form 'Picotee', introduced by Antonelli's in 1954, is known by the contrasting colors of the flowers, as if a darker edge had been painted on the petals.

Shorter, compact plants, good for containers, are a recent development. Bedding or wax begonias, fuchsias, azaleas, camellias, tree ferns, and gloxinias are other specialties. Planting mixes and soil amendments needed for the fast-draining, humus-rich soil begonias require are always in stock.

**Getting There:** Highway 1 south of Santa Cruz toward Monterey; take 41st Avenue exit toward the ocean. Past the Capitola Mall shopping center, turn right on Capitola Road and go to Maciel Avenue. Park in lot.

**Admission:** Free. Open daily 9am to 5pm.

**Facilities:** Restrooms, benches, picnic tables. Handicapped access good.

**Nearby:** Capitola Begonia Festival in September features nautical parade of floats made of begonia flowers in lagoon near Capitola Beach. Call (408) 475-6522 for dates.

# Roses of Yesterday and Today

❀ 802 Brown's Valley Road, Watsonville

This pioneering source of old or "heritage" roses, as well as rare, unusual, and selected modern roses, is down a shady coastal canyon, where, it might seem, roses of any kind would have a difficult time. But the gardens are on rolling slopes where they receive maximum sun and are far enough inland to escape ocean fogs off Monterey Bay.

A family-owned nursery in business since the 1930s, Roses of Yesterday and Today maintains strict grading standards for their stock and gives high priority to customer service. A large part of the business is mail order, and the catalog itself is a collector's item. A brief history of roses, charming descriptions, and sometimes amusing testimonials from growers make reading it a treat.

A walk up the drive to the new office, built after a mudslide in 1982 destroyed the old one down near the creek, takes visitors past three plants of 'Raubritter' planted in a stump. Their clusters of globular, semi-double, pink blooms cascading down a bank always receive attention.

On a south slope below the office noteworthy plants are, to name but a few, 'Maytime', a floribunda shrub rose with large,

*'Raubritter' roses tumble over old stump*

apricot-pink buds shading to creamy coral after opening; 'Prairie Princess', a repeat-blooming shrub rose with long, pointed pink buds and clear pink flowers, good for arrangements; and 'Sparrieshoop', growing up to the balcony as a climber (it grows also as a shrub), with impressive clusters of single, wavy-petaled, pink flowers.

In an area fenced to keep deer out is a large selection of shrub and climbing roses, including 'Belle of Portugal', a vigorous climber to sixteen feet, here rambling up into an old apple tree; and 'Maréchal Niel', with pale yellow, fragrant flowers, twining over another tree. 'Lawrence Johnston', a large shrub or climber, with fragrant, bright yellow flowers, combines nicely with 'Wind Chimes', a prolific bloomer with clusters of fuchsia-pink single flowers with pale centers and clean, pointed leaves. Don't miss 'De Meaux', beside the entrance gate; it is dainty and charming with small, fern-like leaves and tiny, powder-pink buds opening into intensely fragrant flowers with layers of pale to deep pink petals.

**Getting There:** Highway 1 south from Santa Cruz to Freedom Boulevard exit toward foothills. Continue about six miles to Corralitos Road, turn left, and go about two miles to Corralitos Market. Turn right about one-quarter mile to Brown's Valley Road and turn left. Entrance is about 2.5 miles. Park in lot.

**Admission:** Free. Visitors welcome anytime, but sales of roses Monday through Friday 9am to 3pm only.

**Facilities:** Restrooms, benches, picnic tables. Handicapped access limited. Cards, books, catalog at office. Open house and plant sale Mother's Day weekend. For information (408) 724-3537. To order roses (408) 724-2755.

**Nearby:** John Ewing Orchids is on White Road in Watsonville. West on Highway 152 (Hecker Pass Road) is Hecker Pass Family Adventure, with award-winning landscape of native plants and many family-oriented attractions.

# Old Monterey

❀ Wharf to El Dorado Street, Monterey

A walk through the gardens of Old Monterey is a walk through early California history. To see the modern gardens and historic adobes of Old Monterey, start at the Custom House, across from the marina and Fisherman's Wharf, a short walk from the parking lot at Scott and Pacific streets. Pamphlets, books, maps, and tickets for tours are available at the Custom House. The restored adobe building is part of Monterey State Historic Park, as are most of the other old buildings mentioned here.

The Custom House, built in 1827, contains an upstairs museum with rooms furnished as they were in the nineteenth century when duties were collected from foreign ships. The plaza garden consists mostly of succulents and cacti in beds between sandy paths with pepper trees, cypresses, and coast live oaks.

Pacific House, a short walk south, originally was used to store military supplies, and the walled garden was a corral for army horses. Dominated by a hexagonal pool and fountain with large magnolias at four corners, this court is said to have been popular for bull and bear fights. Arched verandas, tiled walls, camellias, roses, an enormous Australian tea tree, wisteria on a trellis of unpeeled logs, and a bed of succulents planted in the shape of a bear make this an amusing garden.

Out the back gate under the arbor, diagonally across Olivier Street, is the Boston Store, featuring old trading items and herbs. The lower portion of the two-level garden is small, sunny, high-walled, and filled with fragrant herbs. Old wine bottles and abalone shells define beds between raked sand paths. From a bench here one can enjoy the mixed scents of aromatic plants and red bougainvillea against a white chimney. It is a few steps to the upper garden with brick patio, paths lined with jade plants, mixed beds of roses, daisies, and hydrangeas, a pepper tree, and comfortable benches with good views. Restrooms here have tile roofs and verandas to blend with the other buildings. Take the side gate to Scott Street, turn left, and walk to the corner of Pacific Street. Cross the street to California's first theater and Jack's Tavern, on the corner.

Go in the side garden gate, on into the tavern, then through the adjoining theater, where performances started about 1848, and out the back door to an old-fashioned garden with two huge cypress trees towering over multi-level beds of fuchsias, ferns, wax begonias, and valerian. Up some stone steps are benches, a bird bath, and raised beds of roses and seasonal flowers. Walk south from here on Pacific Street.

*Sunlight and shadow on bricks at Old Whaling Station*

Casa Soberanes, the House with the Blue Gate, has mixed beds on either side of central steps leading uphill to the two-story house. A wisteria-draped arbor with seats nearly conceals the front door. Succulents, pelargoniums, jade plants, and dusty miller fill beds lined with old bottles. The side path leads to a sunny garden outside the low-roofed kitchen porch. Here fruit trees, grape vines on porch posts, herbs, olive trees, strawberry beds, and a vegetable patch remind us that gardens of old were useful as well as decorative. High walls offer protection from prevailing winds. Take the side gate that lets out on Del Monte Avenue, turn left, and go back down to Pacific Street. Turn right to Jefferson Street, then left to Larkin House.

With its second-story balcony and first-floor verandas, Larkin House, built in the 1830s, is the prototype for Old Monterey architecture. The gardens, surrounded by a high rock wall, have small lawns, tall yews, olives, a strawberry tree, and 'Climbing Cécile Brunner' roses over a long wood arbor. The side garden has carved Mexican benches and a charming antique child's bench set under a redwood tree. Roses by the porch can be seen from the windows of the old house. Go out the low gate in the rear wall to Pacific Street, then cross the street to the large garden on the corner.

Friendly Plaza Gardens and Colton Hall occupy most of this block, facing Pacific. Colton Hall's second-floor assembly hall is restored as it was when the California constitution was debated and drafted here in 1849. The extensive, park-like garden has rock-walled raised beds with roses, fuchsias, and flowering plants. Specimen trees — old apples, olives, oaks, redwoods, magnolias, and liquidambars — grow around wide lawns. Benches, a brick courtyard with rose garden, and a circular rock wall around a large chestnut — a memorial tree, as are many others — give this plaza the air of a public square. Walk south on Pacific Street to the corner of Madison, angle left on Polk, and cross Polk to the gate in a tall wall enclosing a complex of adobe buildings.

The Cooper-Molera Adobes are several buildings dating from the 1820s and 1830s, connected behind old adobe and rock walls, which conceal this almost two-and-one-half-acre site of rural-style gardens, courtyard, and redwood barn built in 1900. A cypress tree believed to be a century old, an ancient walnut, plus other old trees — mission fig, quince, 'Bellflower' and 'Gravenstein' apples, and 'Yellow Egg' plum — set the atmosphere for the gardens. Plants and gardening methods authentic to the 1800s are used in the vegetable garden. Rows of corn, squash, peas, carrots, turnips, and onions are marked with sticks, and crossed twig hoops support peas and other vining plants. Only fertilizers and pest controls of the time are used. An old well, adobe oven (called a *hornito*), outhouse, and farm buildings are preserved. Marigolds, old roses, lavender, sage, and hollyhocks grow here, and pens hold sheep and black Majorca chickens. Artifacts found during excavation and restoration of the site are displayed in the main building. Go out the front gate, continue on Polk to the corner of Munras Avenue, cross the street, and turn right.

Enter the walled, south-facing Stevenson House garden through the gate with tall cypress trees. The residence was a rooming house, and author Robert Louis Stevenson rented a second-story room overlooking the garden in 1879. Several rooms are open to the public, displaying items and keepsakes of Stevenson's life and work. In the sunny rear garden wide sandy paths are edged by bricks, and annuals and perennials, including many herbs, blend well in beds among large trees. Ripe figs and apricots attract crows, blackbirds, and jays. Hummingbirds hover around the fuchsias. Lemon, almond, quince, and plum trees remain from an old orchard. Huge magnolias shade comfortable benches near the house. Go through an open corridor on the ground level to the front garden enclosed by a picket fence. With azaleas, hydrangeas, an enormous fuchsia growing to the second story, and pepper trees, this more traditional, shady garden at the front of the house faces Houston Street. Go out the front gate, turn left on Houston, go to Pearl, then turn left to Alvarado. Turn right and continue on Alvarado. Walk through the Monterey Conference Center Mall, with shops and restaurants, and back to the Custom House. Turn left, go past the First Brick House (under restoration) to the Old Whaling Station.

This old house (not open to the public) was headquarters for the Monterey Whaling Company from the 1850s to the 1880s and a boarding house for Portuguese whalers. The front walk is made of whalebones. A charming side gate in the wall leads to sunny brick walks and a large patio behind the house. Hen-and-chickens succulents line square beds of roses in the side garden, and colorful poppies, phlox, cosmos, and other flowers nod against the enclosing walls. In back is a twisted, shaggy-barked mayten tree. An arbor, with old pear tree above, leads to a small area with narrow walks between maze-like beds lined with rosemary pruned as low hedges. The scent of sweet alyssum and roses floats through the garden. Go out the side gate (notice the bougainvillea espaliered on the wall) and walk across the pedestrian bridge back to the public parking lot on Scott Street.

**Getting There:** Highway 1 to Monterey; take Fremont Street/Monterey Peninsula College exit west. Continue on Fremont to Munras and then to Pacific. Turn right and go to Scott, then turn left to public parking lot or park on street.

**Admission:** Entry to gardens free, and, except for Cooper-Molera Adobes, gardens can be seen without touring buildings. Tickets for guided house tours available at Custom House. Casa Soberanes, Larkin House, Stevenson House, and Cooper-Molera Adobes, all part of Monterey State Historic Park, are open daily 10am to 5pm (4pm in winter). Guided tours on the hour. Adults, $3.50 for all four buildings or $1 each; children 6 to 16 years, $2 for all four or $.50 each. Custom House is free, self-guided. Pacific House charges for self-guided museum tour. Call (408) 649-7118. Colton Hall is a City of Monterey property, open daily 10am to 5pm. Free self-guided tours. Call (408) 375-9944 for group tours.

**Facilities:** Restrooms shown on brochure maps, benches, drinking fountains, gift shops, exhibits. Handicapped access generally excellent.

**Nearby:** Monterey Peninsula Museum of Art is on Pacific Street across from Colton Hall, and Maritime Museum is around corner on Calle Principal. Fisherman's Wharf, Cannery Row, and Monterey Bay Aquarium are blocks away.

# Lester Rowntree Arboretum

❀ 25800 Hatton Road, Carmel

Named for the author, naturalist, and lecturer whose seed-gathering trips throughout California in the 1930s and 1940s brought many native plants to the attention of the horticultural world, this small arboretum in a residential area of Carmel is a cooperative project of the City of Carmel and the Monterey Bay chapter of the California Native Plant Society. Cared for by community volunteers, the garden was created to display California natives that are adaptable to cultivated gardens, with an emphasis on plants that require little or no water.

At the entrance off Hatton Road is a bulletin board with photographs and brochures describing some of the plants to be seen in the garden. The woodsy setting is dominated by Monterey pines, coast live oaks, Monterey cypresses, and Gowen cypresses (*Cupressus goveniana*), a rare tree native to the Monterey peninsula. There are also madrones, redwoods, white alders, and buckeyes. Understory includes native sword ferns, fuchsia-flowering gooseberries, and red-flowering currants. A few blue gum eucalypts and some other non-native plants have been retained from the garden of the estate on which the arboretum was established.

A fine collection of native bulbs blooms in late winter and early spring. Pacific Coast irises flower later. In raised beds on a sunny slope are many brodiaeas and calochortuses. In shaded areas look for the ground-covering foliage of inside-out flower (*Vancouveria hexandra*) and the nodding flowers of western columbine.

Along the path are evergreen tanbark oak, with toothed, leathery leaves; pinyon pine, a slow-growing, small tree with edible seeds; coast silktassel, an excellent evergreen shrub to small tree with pendulous catkins; and the large, shrubby island bush poppy, with clear yellow, poppy-like flowers and gray-green leaves. The acid berries of lemonadeberry can be crushed to flavor drinks.

Near a small lath house is a bench with a fine view of Point Lobos and Carmel Bay through the pines. Among the manzanitas here is a plant named *Arctostaphylos* 'Lester Rowntree'. Like Rowntree, who was barely five feet tall and lived to the age of one hundred, this manzanita is low-growing, close to the earth, sturdy, and long-lived.

Up the slope are several fine specimens of fernleaf Catalina ironwood, an attractive, open-branched tree with shaggy bark and fern-like clusters of leaves. Near these trees is a large stand of buckwheat, among Rowntree's favorite plants. There are also several varieties of striking, blue-flowered ceanothus here, as well as yellow-flowered southern flannel bush, monkeyflowers, and penstemons.

Seeing native plants in a garden setting is a pleasure for those familiar with them and may inspire others to consider natives for their home gardens. Thanks are due to the dedicated lovers of native flora who made the arboretum possible, and to the hard-working volunteers who maintain it.

**Getting There:** Highway 1 to Carmel. Turn toward the ocean at Ocean Avenue, go one block, and turn left on Hatton Road. Entrance on right in about one mile. Park on street.

**Admission:** Free, but donations appreciated. Open daily.

**Facilities:** Benches. Handicapped access limited. Plant sale in October.

**Nearby:** Also in Carmel are Robinson Jeffers' Tor House and restored Carmel mission, built in 1770, with garden and museum of mission relics. Pacific Grove Museum of Natural History, on Forest Avenue in Pacific Grove, features plants and animals of the Monterey Peninsula.

# Tor House

❀ 26304 Ocean View Avenue, Carmel

Framed by Monterey pines and cypresses, Robinson Jeffers' low stone Tor House and Hawk Tower are overwhelmed by adjacent large homes, but climb the narrow tower stairs to the roof-top view of the garden and Carmel Bay and you have some sense of the lonely shore as it was in 1918 when Jeffers and his wife Una began Tor House.

Large granite boulders were hauled to the site, and Jeffers apprenticed himself to the building contractor to learn stone masonry. So skilled was he that he built Hawk Tower in only four years. He wrote, "My fingers had the art to make stone love stone."

Pounding surf, buzzing bees, and the quivering stillness of hummingbirds evoke the feeling of solitude Jeffers must have found

*Pleasing mix of plants gives country-cottage charm*

on this bleak headland. Inspired by the rugged coast, his strong poetry soon brought him renown.

For privacy Jeffers planted pines and eucalypts. Remnants of this grove are still used by nesting night herons. Irish yews, common in England and Ireland, countries especially loved by Mrs. Jeffers and visited by both, were planted years ago. Now they are tall columns, higher than the house. When the house was completed, the Jefferses had light from lamps, heat from fireplaces, no telephone, no houses nearby; just the wildness of the coast, walks to town and beach, writing, reading, piano music — and the planting of a garden. Mrs. Jeffers patterned it after an English garden, and they both tended it. Fences and walls helped protect against wind and sea spray, which also affected their choice of plants. Lavender, rosemary, santolina, rose geranium, lemon verbena, and masses of sweet alyssum and scented purple irises were planted almost seventy years ago. Eighty-six kinds of roses, mostly old varieties and a few highly scented modern ones, have been added in the last forty years, along with vast quantities of small bulbs, especially freesias, babianas, daffodils, and lilies.

Peruvian lilies, daylilies, evening primroses, delphiniums, and other tall flowers peek over a wall. Inside the entry gate a profusion of plants compatible with cool, foggy weather line the walk. The rose 'La Reine Victoria', with pale lilac-pink, semi-double flowers, rambles beside the gate to the beach. 'Belle of Portugal', 'Wind Chimes', 'Joseph's Coat', 'Rosa Mundi', and *Rosa rugosa* 'Alba' are some of the roses near the house.

Outside the dining room a huge Monterey cypress arches over the rock outcropping, called a tor, for which the house is named. Geraniums and nasturtiums spread over the spray-misted slope below herbs — borage, oregano, lavender, sage, fennel, creeping thyme — fragrant in the sun.

In Hawk Tower a motto reads, "They build their dreams themselves." Robinson and Una Jeffers' dream still stands serene on wind-tossed Carmel Bay: a charming stone house set in an old-fashioned garden.

**Getting There:** Highway 1 to Carmel; take Ocean Avenue exit west toward the water. Turn left on Scenic Road, go one mile, and turn left on Stewart Way. At Ocean View Avenue turn left again. Park on street or in driveway.

**Admission:** Adults, $5; college students, $3.50; high-school students, $1.50. No children. Docent-led tours Fridays and Saturdays only 10am to 4pm. Reservations required. Call (408) 624-1840.

**Facilities:** Handicapped access very limited. No restrooms. No photos in house. Gift and book shop. Festival in October; open house garden party in May.

# Barnyard Shopping Center

❀ Carmel Rancho Boulevard, Carmel Valley

With views of misty hills near the Carmel River and the sea, visitors can walk through an attractive garden as they shop. The colorful gardens at Barnyard Shopping Center, easily located by its windmill, were designed to require little maintenance and minimal water. They are a floral bonanza, too.

Undulating terrain was not leveled when nine buildings resembling barns were constructed, making an intimate complex joined by brick walks, steps, bridges, and courtyards. Succulent Gardens Nursery is located in a court at the north end. Fences and gates are hung with succulent wreaths and pictures, a nursery specialty. In a charming setting made for browsing are dish gardens, unusual pottery, dried materials and arrangements, and a varied selection of wind chimes ringing softly in the breeze.

Plantings on slopes and mounds and in secluded pockets change with the seasons, but locations dictate similar plants from year to year. Pelargoniums of every color like the sun, as do Shasta daisies, pansies, California poppies, marguerites, asters, ranunculus and other bulbs, sweet alyssum, lobelia, and gazanias. Plants that appreciate shade and filtered sun include foxgloves, fuchsias, and ferns. There are always gladiolus, lavender, agapanthus, coral bells, tall blue Mexican sage, and bright red bougainvillea against sunny walls.

Purple-leaf plum, ginkgo, and liquidambar trees give fall color, and many drought-tolerant trees and shrubs, such as Australian grevillea, form accents of varying heights between buildings and flower beds. Honeysuckle and white-flowered potato vine twine up posts and railings, filling the air with pleasant scents. Visitors stroll the paths, stopping to rest on benches from which the garden can be enjoyed or to smell and admire the flowers.

**Getting There:** Highway 1 to Carmel Valley Road exit east; turn right on Carmel Rancho Boulevard. Park in lot.

**Admission:** Shops open 10am to 5pm in winter, 10am to 8pm in summer.

**Facilities:** Benches, restrooms, drinking fountains. Handicapped access limited. The shopping center has varied shops and restaurants, including bookstore/cafe with greenhouse dining area overlooking gardens.

**Nearby:** More shops, restaurants, golf courses, Carmel mission, Monterey's Cannery Row, and the Monterey Bay Aquarium are all close by.

# Carmel Valley Begonia Gardens

❀ 9920 Carmel Valley Road, Carmel Valley

Carmel Valley Begonia Gardens, right off busy Carmel Valley Road, is a quiet retreat in a woodsy setting. This nursery offers much more than begonias, and it is well worth a visit any time of year. Dozens and dozens of pots, on tables in the courtyard entrance and inside, introduce the visitor to one of this nursery's claims to fame: colorful flowering plants. Whatever is in season is here in abundance — primroses, violets, pansies, cyclamens, azaleas, chrysanthemums, daisies.

Greenhouses devoted to pelargoniums and scented geraniums are a sea of pink, red, rose, and soft orange. Another greenhouse contains a variety of house plants, including orchids and unusual ivies and ferns. In late fall and winter a large area is given over to bare-root and potted roses suited to the climate of coastal California. Also available are bromeliads, hydrangeas, camellias, decorative grasses, many kinds of citrus, ornamentally trained shrubs, flowering vines, and a good selection of bulbs.

The special attraction is, of course, tuberous begonias. The place glows with them, hanging everywhere, arrayed on tables and benches, begonias in an explosion of color, with ruffled, scalloped, smooth, and layered blossoms — an unforgettable sight. Come in summer (mid-July to late August is peak flowering time) to experience this horticultural treat.

**Getting There:** Highway 1 south of Carmel. Take the Carmel Valley Road exit and go about six miles east to nursery. Park in lot.

**Admission:** Free. Open Thursday through Tuesday 9am to 5pm. For information call (408) 624-7231.

**Facilities:** Restrooms, benches. Handicapped access good.

**Nearby:** At the junction of Carmel Valley Road and Highway 1 stroll through the multi-level landscape of Barnyard Shopping Center to enjoy a seasonal array of plants. Thunderbird Book Shop has a feast of books and a greenhouse lunch room. Carmel mission is across Highway 1, and the quaint shops and streets of Carmel are a few blocks away. Tor House, home of poet Robinson Jeffers, is on Ocean View Avenue in Carmel.

# Orchid Garden Nursery

❀ 33 Los Robles Drive, Carmel Valley

Down Carmel Valley Road, past shopping centers, golf courses, horse ranches, and suburban homes, is a paradise of orchids. Set in a complex of rustically styled modern buildings along a country lane lined with oaks are the greenhouses and nursery of Kit Kurz, orchid breeder and proprietor of The Orchid Garden, a retail orchid nursery.

Kurz started with one plant, and like gardeners and plant lovers everywhere, found that one orchid led to more; she now has over 10,000. Hers is the only retail orchid nursery in Monterey County, and she welcomes visitors.

Her favorites are the epiphytic moth orchids (*Phalaenopsis*), which grow high in the branches of trees in tropical or subtropical jungles, but she offers many other kinds of orchids too. Some flower for only a few weeks, others for many months. Peak flowering is from early spring through mid-October, but there is never a time when no plants are in bloom.

Kurz says phalaenopsis orchids prefer indirect light and adapt easily to the home environment, providing months of flowers in a multitude of hues. Knowledgeable and helpful to newcomers

*Flowers of moth orchid in graceful spray*

who know little about orchids, she guides visitors to plants that will give the most enjoyment for their home conditions. If you can leave without buying an orchid, your powers of resistance must be very great indeed, or your wallet very thin.

**Getting There:** Highway 1 south past Carmel; turn left at Carmel Valley Road exit and go 8.5 miles, turn left on Miramonte Road and go three-quarters of a mile, then turn right on Los Robles Drive. Park in front.

**Admission:** Open Tuesday through Friday 10am to 3pm, Saturday and Sunday 10am to 5pm.

**Facilities:** Display area, benches, brochures. Handicapped access limited in greenhouses. Call (408) 659-3940.

**Nearby:** Continue east on Carmel Valley Road to the village, with shops and restaurants, or go back toward Highway 1 and stop at Barnyard Shopping Center to see the lovely landscape, with succulent nursery, shops, and eating places. Point Lobos State Park, with hiking trails and picnic areas, is a few miles south off Highway 1.

## Also of Interest

**John Ewing Orchids,** 487 White Road, Watsonville (408) 684-1111. Wide selection of orchids for beginners and collectors. Classes, lectures, open houses, special sales; catalog packed with information.

# Central Valley/Gold Country

# 5.

# Micke Grove Japanese Garden

❀ 11793 North Micke Grove Park Road, Lodi

If driving through the valley on Highway 5 becomes tiresome, turn off at Eight Mile Road between Stockton and Lodi and rest body and spirit at the Japanese garden in Micke Grove Park.

The oak-studded land for the county park was set aside by farsighted resident William G. Micke, who valued the groves of native trees. In the park is a three-acre gem of a Japanese garden, given by generous San Joaquin County residents of Japanese ancestry. Trees and shrubs were contributed by individuals and nurseries both locally and throughout the state.

Entry to the garden is through a Japanese-style gate, accented on each side by flower beds, low pines, and large rocks. Straight ahead is a teahouse, a beautiful structure of natural wood, harmonious with the surrounding oak trees. A grassy area in front of the teahouse is used for weddings and other events. Luncheons are often held inside.

A winding path inside the gate leads to a camellia garden where hundreds of these shade-loving plants enjoy filtered light under mature oaks. Weeping cherry trees and many azaleas here add to the spring flower feast.

*Horizontally trained pine tree reflected in pond*

Wide asphalt paths off the central walkway meander among irregular beds. A variety of trees and shrubs, including camellias, azaleas, junipers, pyracanthas, and cotoneasters, give the visual effect of layers of texture and tones of green. Steppingstones beside a path lead to a small, black pagoda. Nandina, irises, podocarpus, and large pyracantha bushes form a background for the delicate structure.

A low footbridge across a free-form pond gives good views of islands planted with junipers, azaleas, and pines. Boulders and bamboo form a transition at the rock-cobbled shore. A bridge with red railings is a good place to watch koi fish.

A hill mound features a stone pagoda on the highest point with long views of the garden. Water splashes from a brook down to the pond. A steppingstone path leads to a waterside terrace of dark, smooth stones. A massive stone lantern is placed under alders and birches; bamboo, acanthus, and cotoneaster droop over the tranquil water.

Red-leaf Japanese maples and several large ginkgo trees among oaks near the teahouse make this garden, lovely in any season, especially colorful in fall.

**Getting There:** Highway 5 to Eight Mile Road exit east (between Stockton and Lodi); go about six miles to Micke Grove Park Road, turn left, and go about two miles. Follow signs to Japanese Garden and adjacent parking lot.

**Admission:** $2 per automobile weekdays, $3 weekends and holidays. Park open daily 8am to sunset; garden open weekdays 10am to 4pm, weekends 9am to 2pm.

**Facilities:** Micke Grove Park has restrooms, benches, drinking fountains, picnic tables, barbecues, playfields, children's playground, horseshoe grounds, amusement rides, snack bar, zoo, museum. Handicapped access excellent. Call (209) 331-7400 or 953-8800. County historical museum in park open Wednesday through Sunday 1 to 5pm.

**Nearby:** King's Mums is on Liberty Road in Clements, between Lodi and Stockton.

# U.C. Davis Arboretum

❀ University of California, Davis

Early settlers described the Sacramento Valley as a park because of the many magnificent oaks. Today the University Arboretum at Davis, a 110-acre, two-mile-long strip of land on both sides of Putah Creek, has hundreds of oaks and thousands of other trees, shrubs, and perennials suited to the hot-summer, foggy-winter climate of the interior valley.

From the many entry ways into this unfenced arboretum paths lead along the creek banks, where ancient oaks, redbuds, toyons, buckeyes, bladderpod, and western chokecherry grow. Ducks and geese paddle in the slow-moving water. Large agaves, mesquites, palms, and cacti crowd the desert area. Come to the Mary Wattis Brown Garden of California Native Plants in spring and early summer to see ceanothus, manzanita, bush poppy, wild rose, buckwheat, currants, golden lupine, California poppies, and other native plants in bloom.

The T. Elliot Weier Redwood Grove is the largest outside the coastal fog belt. There are also important collections of plants from South Africa, the Mediterranean, and Australia, including a eucalyptus grove of over seventy species. Across one of several foot-

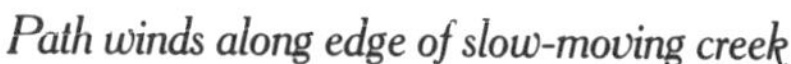

*Path winds along edge of slow-moving creek*

bridges, a path on the south bank is lined with acacias, with blooms that create a fragrant, golden cloud in spring. Further west, above the south bank, California black walnuts provide shade for benches and picnic tables near Putah Creek lodge. Up the slope a sunny knoll overlooks the creek.

Special gardens in the west area include the Carolee Shields White Flower Garden, sometimes called a moon garden because the white flowers of vines and shrubs are visible at night, when fragrance also intensifies. An annual moonlight walk begins here at the time of the full moon in late spring.

The Ruth Risdon Storer Garden features low-maintenance, water-conserving perennials and small shrubs. This charming garden has winding paths separating beds planted with rosemary, artemisias, lavenders, salvias, Russian sage, scabiosa, sedums, bulbs, Chinese plumbago, California fuchsia, rock roses, and many other plants that are drought-resistant and easy to grow.

The Peter J. Shields Oak Grove is a fifteen-acre stand of eighty different kinds of oaks from California and around the world. Attached to the arboretum is a riparian reserve of some 300 acres bordering another part of the creek. In 1988 over a hundred valley oaks were planted as part of a restoration project in that area. The endangered Swainson's hawk and elderberry longhorn beetle find refuge in the lush woodlands. Twenty species of fish swim in the year-round stream.

Environmental education is an important part of the arboretum's conservation efforts, and school children are frequent visitors. An outdoor education program sponsored by the arboretum teaches young people to appreciate and enjoy the natural world so that they will become "responsible stewards of the earth." Whatever your age, this arboretum is a place for education and enjoyment.

**Getting There:** Highway 80 west of Sacramento; take U.C. Davis exit (Old Davis Road) and continue to campus. Across bridge turn left on La Rue Road and go past arboretum office on left. Park in metered lot.

**Admission:** Free. Open daily. Office open Monday through Friday 8am to noon and 1 to 5pm, except holidays.

**Facilities:** Restroom near office, drinking fountains, benches, picnic tables. Handicapped access good. Pamphlets, books, maps for sale at office. Lodge may be reserved for events; call (916) 752-1920. Picnic areas also may be reserved; call (916) 752-2813. Plant sales behind office for Friends of the Davis Arboretum first Thursday, November through June, 10am to 12:30pm (you may join at door). Public plant sale first Saturday after fall classes start; moonlight walk in late spring; lecture series; Sunday arboretum tours. Call (916) 752-2498 or 752-4880.

# Capitol Park

❀ Downtown Sacramento

Each year thousands of people from throughout the United States and the world visit the golden-domed state capitol building and its forty-acre landscape, with trees and shrubs from many continents and climates and special gardens of roses, camellias, and cacti. The park is a haven for squirrels and an arboreal oasis for legislators, government workers, and nature lovers, who eat, talk, and watch other people from the many benches beside the paths.

Visitors may take a self-guided walk or join a guided tour at the office in the basement of the capitol building. Each tour differs, depending on the guide and what visitors wish to see. Tour guides can answer questions about the history of the buildings and the original plantings between Tenth and Eleventh streets, including stone pines and deodar cedars planted in 1872. Park records do not indicate whether the grand old southern magnolias also were planted at that time.

There is a trout pond, a memorial to veterans of the Spanish-American War, and a memorial grove of trees, some of which were transplanted as saplings in 1897 from Civil War battlefields. A replica of the Liberty Bell and a bell from the U.S.S. California, the only World War II battleship built on the West Coast, are also here. The path leads to a statue of Father Junipero Serra, founder of the California missions, then to a camellia grove dedicated to early settlers of California. Hundreds of camellias bloom in late winter through March, when the Sacramento Camellia Festival is celebrated. Enormous English elms, planted in 1882, alternate with Washington fan palms along an old carriage drive. In this area many deciduous trees, including a huge chestnut oak from Appomattox, Virginia, give good fall color.

A small cactus garden is set in a section of California native plants, many of which were sent by school children to Governor Hiram Johnson in 1914. An extensive rose garden, with hundreds of varieties, is close by. The American Rose Society uses these beds to test roses each year.

There are magnificent magnolias near Twelfth and L streets, and giant sequoias at Thirteenth and L. A visit in early spring to see peonies and camellias in bloom gives the added bonus of dogwoods, magnolias, and other flowering trees at their best.

**Getting There:** Highway 80 in Sacramento to Business 80 east; exit on Sixteenth Street, go north to L Street, and turn left. Park and capitol bounded by L and N streets and Tenth and Sixteenth streets. Park on street or in public lots nearby.

**Admission:** Grounds open daily. Tours are free. Capitol closed major holidays.

**Facilities:** Restrooms, benches, drinking fountains. Handicapped access excellent. For tour information call (916) 324-0333. Books, maps, pamphlets at tour office.

**Nearby:** Sutter's Fort, the first European outpost in California's interior valley, and the State Indian Museum are east of Capitol Park at 28th and L streets. McKinley Park, with art and garden center, many roses and camellias, small duck pond, horseshoe grounds, and picnic areas, is on Alhambra Avenue east of Capitol Park. Old Sacramento, a ten-block restoration project with many shops and restaurants, is between Highway 5 and the Sacramento River on Embarcadero. The State Railroad Museum is in Old Sacramento between Second and I streets.

# Goethe Arboretum

❀ 6000 J Street, Sacramento

Tucked between busy J Street and a shady parking lot on the campus of California State University, this small, park-like arboretum is easily overlooked. The arboretum is named for the late Charles M. Goethe, Sacramento resident and "friend of man and nature."

Asphalt paths are wide and comfortable for strolling. A circular bed with large rocks, stone bench, and sundial is filled with drought-tolerant plants. The gray-green leaves and paper-like, white flowers of the native matilija poppy are prominent in summer. In this area also are a small South American tree (*Schinus polygamus*), related to the commonly cultivated and much larger California pepper tree (*S. molle*), and Chinese pistache trees, with dense, fern-like foliage that puts on an outstanding display of orange and red in fall.

A variety of blue elderberry from Southern California and desert states (known as *neomexicana*) has grayer leaves and smaller berries than the Northern California roadside plant but the same whitish powdery "bloom" on the pale blue fruits. Birds love both of them.

A bulletin board near the center of the arboretum has a map with a numbered plant list. Beside the board is a slow-growing evergreen corokia, which does well in alkaline soil; its interlaced, contorted, nearly black branches are sparsely covered with glossy green leaves and tiny yellow flowers. Nearby are deciduous empress trees, tropical-looking with large, heart-shaped leaves and fragrant clusters of lavender flowers in spring.

Among other notable trees are a large tulip tree, a double-trunked California bay laurel, and a wide-spreading camphor tree. The broad branches of the camphor make a good resting spot, out of hot sun, for California gray squirrels.

Two deciduous, shrubby plants, good for home gardens, are Chinese witch hazel, which has fragrant, golden yellow flowers that bloom on bare branches from December to March; and a mock orange (*Philadelphus argyrocalyx*), whose flat, white flowers have a spicy, citrus-like fragrance.

At the southwest end of the arboretum is a collection of drought-tolerant native trees and shrubs. A large iris garden, established in memory of Lloyd Austin for hybridizing work at the Institute of Forest Genetics, is most colorful in mid-spring.

**Getting There:** Highway 50 east of Sacramento toward South Lake Tahoe; exit at Howe Avenue north. Follow Howe to

Fair Oaks Boulevard, turn left, and go about one mile. Where J Street and H Street separate, bear left on J about one-quarter mile to university entrance. Turn right on Jordan Way. Arboretum is on right. Park in metered lot.

**Admission:** Free. Open daily all year.

**Facilities:** Benches, picnic tables. Handicapped access good. Restrooms across parking lot and across street at administration building (open weekdays 7:30am to 5pm and Saturdays 9am to 1pm).

**Nearby:** State capitol building and surrounding park, restored buildings and shops of Old Sacramento, State Railroad Museum, and Sutter's Fort with State Indian Museum are all nearby.

# Fountain Square Nursery

❀ 7115 Greenback Lane, Citrus Heights

Built around and integrated with a shopping center in the Sacramento suburbs, Fountain Square Heritage Rose Nursery specializes in roses but also offers plants for shade and unusual specimen plants. Visitors walk through the nursery to get to the Trellis Cafe, where the fragrance of roses and flowering vines and the cool splash of water make luncheon a memorable event. Past the cafe is a courtyard with a fountain and roses planted in symmetrical beds. Shops and offices look out on or open onto the flower-filled court and planted beds.

Japanese maples frame the gate to an All-American Rose Selection test garden behind the courtyard, where hundreds of varieties in dozens of beds are grown in an open field. Peak blooming for roses in the Sacramento area is late April through May, although some plants bloom all summer, and some put on a second show in fall.

Unusual roses offered at the nursery include "micro-mini" cascading roses, with small leaves, tiny flowers, and cascading growth habit. Beautiful examples of these plants are displayed on pedestals to show them off at their best. An impressive variety of

*Ornate fountain is focal point of symmetrical rose beds*

other kinds of roses is available in boxes and cans.

The nursery has a diverse selection of camellias, azaleas, rhododendrons, ferns, and other shade plants. Also offered are bonsai starts, hanging baskets and dish gardens, and plants pruned into pyramids, balls, columns, squares, and other shapes, as well as espaliered on trellises and twining on posts or arbors. Statuary, fountains, bird baths, over-sized pots and urns, and garden ornaments of many kinds help gardeners choose containers and accompaniments to enhance their plants.

According to nursery proprietor Katherine Kroeger, the land occupied by the nursery has been in the family for more than a hundred years. No longer in agricultural crops, the Kroeger ranch today serves the community in a different way. Besides selling plants, it is a center for gardeners in the area, providing rose pruning demonstrations, judged flower shows, annual offerings of chrysanthemum cuttings (along with advice for planting), and a large selection of display and test roses to study.

**Getting There:** Highway 80 east of Sacramento to Greenback Lane exit east nearly four miles to nursery near the intersection of Greenback and Sunrise Boulevard. Park in lot.

**Admission:** Open daily 9am to 6pm.

**Facilities:** Restrooms. Handicapped access good. Cafe open Monday through Saturday 11am to 2:30pm, Sunday 10:30am to 2:30pm. Rose pruning demonstrations in January Saturdays and Sundays noon to 2pm. Judged rose show in May, mini-rose show in September, chrysanthemum show in October. Chrysanthemum cuttings available May and June. For information call (916) 969-6666.

**Nearby:** One of three locations of Capitol Nurseries is on Sunrise Boulevard in Citrus Heights. Or continue east on Greenback Lane to the State Recreation Area at the American River and to Folsom Lake, with trails, picnicking, boating, swimming. Ancil Hoffman County Park at the east end of Palm Avenue (off Fair Oaks Boulevard) in Carmichael has a nature center, picnicking under large oaks, playfields, and public golf course.

# Jensen Botanical Garden

❀ Fair Oaks Boulevard, Carmichael

This garden was established by Charles C. Jensen, a World War I pilot and one of the founders of the Daedalians, a fraternity of aviators. He owned a nursery in Oakland until 1958, when he bought three and one-half acres of blackberry vines and pasture in Carmichael, a Sacramento suburb. He and his family brought many plants from Oakland in a caravan of cars and trucks, including magnolias, azaleas, dogwoods, and Japanese maples. Thus began the garden that is now operated by the Carmichael Parks and Recreation Department.

A huge valley oak and a small seasonal creek with wooden bridge mark the entrance to the garden, and many other oak trees provide shady relief on hot summer days. Earth and gravel walks wind through a woodland along a creek, where Japanese irises, orange daylilies, and ferns provide color and texture. Small decks and a gazebo overlook the creek. Many of the 900 azaleas and more than one hundred rhododendrons that were part of the original garden are still thriving.

Coast redwoods were growing on the site when the Jensens came to Carmichael, and a dawn redwood (*Metasequoia glypto-*

*Tree-shaded flower bed extends into lawn*

*stroboides*), acquired only five years after the tree's discovery in China in 1944, was brought to the property later. It is said to be equal to specimens found in major botanical gardens in the United States. Another unusual tree is the tall dove tree (*Davidia involucrata*), also native to China. Its large white flowers in May are said to resemble white doves resting on the branches.

Jensen enjoyed showing people around the garden and through the nursery and lath house. The garden was a favorite place for parties, picnics, and weddings. The large, sloping lawn, surrounded by trees, is a natural setting for gatherings and a good place to spread a picnic lunch.

After his death the property was saved from development by a group of citizens who formed the Charles C. Jensen Botanical Garden organization. The parks department assumed ownership in 1976, assuring that future generations will continue to enjoy this charming family garden.

**Getting There:** Highway 80 east of Sacramento to Madison Avenue east. Continue to Manzanita Avenue, turn right, and go to Fair Oaks Boulevard, then turn left and go about a mile to Marshall Street. Entrance sign on right. Park in lot.

**Admission:** Free. Open daily 7am to dark.

**Facilities:** Restrooms, benches, drinking fountain. Handicapped access limited. No pets, no sound amplification, no ball games. Professional photographers must obtain permit from parks department (916) 485-5322.

**Nearby:** Fountain Square Heritage Rose Nursery, with cafe and shops, as well as a large display of All-American Rose Selection test roses, is on Greenback Lane in Citrus Heights.

# Daffodil Hill

❀ 18310 Ram's Horn Grade, Volcano

The rolling 540-acre ranch and six-acre garden called Daffodil Hill was once a way station for travelers and teamsters coming from Kit Carson Pass over the road now known as State Highway 88. The original owner of the property, from Holland, planted daffodils to remind himself of his home country, and subsequent owners tended and expanded the garden. The present owners, Arthur Lucot and his sister Mary Lucot Ryan, continue to maintain and enlarge the now thriving operation, planting up to 5,000 new bulbs each year. Today there are over 250,000 daffodils, jonquils, tulips, narcissus, snowdrops, bluebells, and other flowering bulbs, with hundreds of varieties represented. Thousands of visitors flock to the garden during the spring blooming season.

It is best to come early to enjoy morning sun on the colorful blooms, as well as the relative quiet before the paths are filled with visitors. The hum of bees in flowering apple trees is like a softly murmured song. The sweet fragrance of lilacs floats over sun-drenched slopes, and the air is filled with the sounds of woodpeckers, blue jays, and roosters.

Old picket fences, stone walls, and an original barn and bunk

*Daffodils brighten woodland path*

house are part of the picturesque rural setting. Wood steps and ramps provide access to different levels. Used containers of astonishing variety — teapots, wheelbarrows, kitchen sinks, half barrels, iron pots, tires, wooden boxes — are filled with flowers and placed in corners, under trees, anywhere there is space for more blooms. A large wood planter is bursting with tulips named for famous people and places — 'Hollywood', 'President Kennedy', 'Princess Margaret Rose'.

Long picnic tables and benches on clean-swept soil are placed under walnut trees near the entrance, and many visitors bring picnic lunches. Gold pans and picks, farm wagons, plows, and other old farm implements add interest for nostalgia buffs. Children enjoy the caged rabbits, doves, and chickens and the elusive peacocks, which roam the ranch, piercing the clear air with their startling, loud cries.

A spring trip to Daffodil Hill is a good way to recover from the winter doldrums. Great wealth was taken from the hills of this Gold Rush area. The visitor to Daffodil Hill can return home with the memory of golden flowers nodding in the breeze, a nugget of remembrance to be pulled out and enjoyed over and over again.

**Getting There:** From near Stockton take Highway 88 east through Jackson to village of Pine Grove. Follow signs to Volcano and Daffodil Hill. Park in lot across from entrance.

**Admission:** Free, but donations appreciated. Open daily mid-March to mid-April 9am to 5pm. Call (209) 296-7048 for information.

**Facilities:** Restrooms, picnic tables, benches. Most paths accessible to handicapped.

**Nearby:** Indian Grinding Rocks State Historic Park is on the road to Daffodil Hill. It has native American structures, hiking trails, rock outcroppings used for grinding acorns, and a campground, with a fee for day use as well as for overnight. The town of Volcano has picturesque Gold Rush buildings, ruins, and artifacts.

# Auburn Library

❀ 350 Nevada Street, Auburn

The Auburn-Placer County Library complex has two courtyard gardens and a pleasing landscape designed to accommodate cultural and community events. A triangular court called the Children's Garden is enclosed by a white brick wall on one side and pines and pyracanthas on another. Windows of the children's section of the library look out on rose bushes colorful in bloom against the wall and spreading mimosa trees that shade wooden benches. An amusing rhinoceros sculpture grazes on a small grassy plot, and a rusty metal goat with long horns reaches out as if to munch miniature red roses in a planter box.

A second courtyard flanks the south wing, where floor-to-ceiling windows open onto a tranquil space. An arbor decked with wisteria and jasmine screens long benches underneath from bright sun. Opposite the benches is a small pool ringed by Japanese maples, podocarpus, and agapanthus. This is a quiet place to read, rest, or eat lunch. A gate opens onto a path leading to the back of the building and another landscape.

In a large lawn area a path on the brow of the hill invites visitors down to picnic tables and benches, where native oaks and

*Whimsical rhinoceros sculpture grazes on grassy plot*

digger pines give shade. This enjoyable, park-like garden, sometimes used for garden parties and other events, has a grove of dogwoods, a commemorative bird bath, good views of surrounding hills, and many flowers, changing with the season.

South of the building is the Garden Theater, developed by the Friends of the Library and community service groups. Steps lead down to a grassy, fan-shaped bowl where pillows and blankets are spread to enjoy plays and musical performances. Long beds along the ridge above the theater bowl, between the flights of steps, contain redwoods, crape myrtles, ginkgoes, and olives underplanted with bright annuals and flowering shrubs. Pathside down the slope rows of flowering cherries and western larches bring both spring and fall interest.

**Getting There:** Highway 80 through Sacramento to Auburn; take Maple Street exit and turn left, go over freeway on overpass, turn right on Nevada Street. Park in lot.

**Admission:** Open Monday and Friday 10am to 6pm, Tuesday through Thursday 10am to 9pm, Saturday 9am to 1pm. Closed Sunday.

**Facilities:** Restrooms, benches, drinking fountains, picnic tables. Handicapped access good. For information call (916) 823-4391.

**Nearby:** Auburn has restored buildings from Gold Rush era. Placer County Historical Museum, on fairgrounds off High Street, has a fine collection of Gold Rush artifacts. Shannon-Knox House, with garden, is east of Auburn on Highway 193 in Georgetown.

# Bourn Cottage

❀ 10791 East Empire Street, Grass Valley

Bourn Cottage was built in 1897 by Mr. and Mrs. William Bourn, Jr., for use on visits to inspect the operations of Bourn's Empire Mine, the most productive gold mine in California, with shafts penetrating to a depth of one mile. In addition to Bourn Cottage and a mansion in San Francisco, the Bourns were the owners of Filoli, their summer residence in Woodside. Empire Mine and Bourn Cottage are now a state historic park.

If you can arrange it, visit the garden at Bourn Cottage when the roses are in bloom. 'Gold of Ophir', introduced in 1845, is the earliest of the many old roses here to flower. In peak bloom it covers the arbor behind the manor-style cottage with a fragrant blanket of pinkish gold flowers that fade to dusty yellow.

Brick paths and steps lead from the cottage to terraces planted with many roses. Some historic ones are gallicas, offspring of the oldest cultivated European roses, and damasks, also dating from ancient times. In beds between brick walls and English holly hedges are more recent albas, centifolias, mosses, Bourbons, and hybrid perpetuals. Plants are grouped by date of origin, illustrating how roses have developed over the years.

A master plan for the rose garden and thirteen-acre landscape was prepared by San Francisco architect Willis Polk, who also designed the residence. Over the years some of the original roses died or were removed, and the arbor collapsed. Restoration, begun in the early 1980s, now includes about 950 roses of fifty-six varieties. Some bloom only once a year, usually in late spring, but others, such as disease- and pest-resistant rugosas, bloom continuously, nearly until frost.

Daffodils, old-fashioned purple irises, hollyhocks, gladioli, and annuals brighten terraced beds below the roses. A vegetable garden laid out as it was during the Bourns' ownership is on the lowest terrace. Gardeners plant corn, beans, tomatoes, and greens, as well as sunflowers for the birds.

Reclaiming old and overgrown plants is an ongoing project. Many spireas, viburnums, and forsythias have been restored from the original garden, and an enormous pyracantha has been trimmed to show off its gnarled trunks. Also from the original garden are weigelas, escallonias, a large mock orange with fragrant white flowers on cascading branches, and English hawthorns with clusters of rose-pink flowers. A double row of red maples south of the house matches similar trees on the north side. Among many trees planted years ago are beech, redwood, red horsechestnut, American chestnut, and amur cork (*Phellodendron amurense*) from China.

*Roses grouped by date of origin in terraced beds*

The west terrace of the house has views of two round pools set in wide lawns backed by holly oaks, sweet gums, ginkgoes, and ponderosa pines. A channel steps down the slope, carrying water to a large, angular pool accented by tall Italian cypresses. A path leads to a grassy sward lined with maples, colorful in autumn.

**Getting There:** Highway 80 through Sacramento to Auburn, then Highway 49 to Grass Valley. Exit at Empire Street (Highway 20) east and go about 1.5 miles. Park in lot.

**Admission:** Adults, $1; ages 6 to 17 years, $.50; under 6, free. Open daily 9am to 6pm in summer, 10am to 5pm in winter.

**Facilities:** Restrooms, picnic tables in parking area. Handicapped access good. Slide show or film on Gold Rush history and Empire Mine hourly, 10:30am to 3:30pm. Small museum, gift shop, books, pamphlets. Living History Days six times a year noon to 4pm spring to fall. Mine buildings and mine shaft open to public. Miners' picnic in summer. Holiday open house in November. Call (916) 273-7714 or 273-8522.

**Nearby:** Northstar Mine Powerhouse Museum (Pelton Wheel Museum), on Mill Street across Highway 49 on Allison Ranch Road, has mining artifacts.

# Chinese Temple Garden

❀ 1500 Broderick Street, Oroville

The Oroville Chinese Temple dates from 1863 when it was built to serve a community of 10,000 Chinese laborers. In 1907, following a major flood, most of the Chinese community left Oroville, and the Chan family assumed responsibility for the temple. In 1937 the property was deeded to the City of Oroville, and the temple was opened to the public in 1949. The courtyard and gardens were developed in 1968.

There are three chapels or sanctuaries, one for Taoists, another for Confucians, and a third for Buddhists. The complex of buildings and gardens is a place for quiet meditation.

The gardens were not designed to imitate an existing Chinese garden, but plants and materials common in traditional Chinese gardens are used. The brick temple buildings, which face the Feather River levee, are set in a large lawn. A dwarf pomegranate hedge in front, tall locusts at the entrance, a grove of ginkgo trees, and many trees-of-heaven (*Ailanthus altissima*), native to China, bring shade in summer and colorful leaves in autumn. The hardy trees-of-heaven were often planted in the late 1800s in the gold country because they tolerate hot winds, extreme temperatures, and poor soil. Since then they have seeded themselves prolifically.

Inside, a paved court is framed by an elaborate arbor with wood beams finished in Chinese design. A trellis on one side of the temple supports fragrant jasmine and blue wisteria. Wood benches beside an oriental-style black fence and arbor overlook a small pool surrounded by azaleas, dogwood trees, and camellias. Waterlilies, lotuses, and bronze cranes decorate the still water. A huge old fig tree, black locusts, and a dawn redwood (the deciduous *Metasequoia glyptostroboides*, unrelated to California's native redwood) grow behind the pool and fence.

Across the court from the temple is a tapestry hall, where priceless weavings, parasols, and other artifacts are exhibited. Its entrance is accented by large planter boxes with specimen azaleas. Kiwi vines twine up posts to the second story. A display hall features pottery, bronzes, and other Chinese art objects, and three-dimensional puppets from Oroville's Chinese Opera Theatre are exhibited to suggest a performance in progress.

Tall timber bamboo, symbol of friendship and longevity, lines a passageway leading to a small house typical of those occupied by Chinese workers in the 1860s. Pines, symbols of strength and solitude, loquat, persimmon, flowering peach and apricot, and pomelo grapefruit, with thick-skinned fruit that matures at New Year's, are other symbolic plants.

Peonies, flowering plum trees, Chinese pistache, and Chinese flame trees also grow in this serene garden. Closed off to the world outside its gates, the garden is a mystery from outside but a place of shelter and tranquility within. Fragrant vines and bright leaves in autumn offer tantalizing glimpses of beauty to passersby.

**Getting There:** Highway 5 north from Sacramento to Highway 20 east at Colusa to Highway 70 north at Marysville. In Oroville exit at Montgomery Street east (name changes to Oro Dam Boulevard) and turn left on First Avenue. Go two blocks to Broderick Street and turn right. Park on street or in lot.

**Admission:** Adults, $1.50; children under 12, free. Open Thursday through Monday 11am to 4:30pm; Tuesday and Wednesday 1 to 4:30pm.

**Facilities:** Restrooms, drinking fountain, benches. Handicapped access limited. Photographs prohibited inside temple. For information call (916) 538-2496.

**Nearby:** Follow green line painted on Montgomery Street/Oro Dam Boulevard, a historic trail, to Charles Lott House in Sank Park, fish hatchery, and Oroville Dam on Kelley Ridge Road, which dead-ends at visitors center parking lot. For tours of power house of one of world's largest earth dams call (916) 534-2436.

# Charles Lott House

❀ 1067 Montgomery Street, Oroville

This charming Victorian residence, built in 1856 and beautifully restored, was home to the family of lawyer (later judge) Charles F. Lott. Although Charles, Jr., never married, his sister Cornelia did, but only after her father and brother had died. It is believed that the romantic words on a plaque on the wisteria-covered arbor in front of the house were Cornelia's to Jesse Sank, who waited many years to marry her: "In commemoration of a kiss and promise given between these columns." The mixed fragrances of roses and wisteria seem to echo the sweet vow.

Many features of the garden were put in by Jesse to please Cornelia, and he willed the property to the City of Oroville in her memory. Now known as Sank Park, the historic site covers one square block and includes the Lott home and gardens as well as an old barn and other restored buildings. The picnic tables for public use were a stipulation of Jesse Sank's gift.

Citrus trees that shade patio and picnic tables — sweet oranges (grown from cuttings from John Bidwell's ranch in Chico), grapefruits, and lemons — are remnants of a large orchard. Other trees grown for family use are walnut, loquat, plum, pear, pecan,

*Old lamps light entrance to Victorian house*

and persimmon, some of them very old. This was a family garden, with vegetables, herbs, and cutting beds, as well as a formal landscape designed to express the prosperity of the owners.

Formal features of the garden, in addition to the arbored front walk, include a rose garden enclosed by brick walks, symmetrical flower beds bordered by pruned hedges, a trellised gazebo, and wide lawns with beautiful specimen trees. The gazebo and lawn invited outdoor activities of the time such as croquet and other games, picnics, reading, and writing letters.

Shrubs widely planted in Victorian gardens include snowball viburnums, hydrangeas, camellias, geraniums, and fragrant gardenias. An old water pump from a cistern is placed in a circle of azaleas. Dogwoods and native redbuds shade a white bench. Several kinds of magnolias and hedges of escallonia and India hawthorn bloom along with the azaleas and camellias in early spring. English ivy and yellow-flowered creeping St. Johnswort also survive from the original garden. Other plants, including hybrid roses and a hedge of rock roses, reflect the garden's reconstruction in the late 1960s. The blending of old and new is harmonious, and the garden today is ideal for strolling, sitting, and for more formal gatherings and events.

**Getting There:** Highway 5 north about an hour past Sacramento; take Highway 20 east exit at Colusa. Continue to Highway 70 at Marysville, then north on Highway 70 to Oroville and exit at Montgomery Street east. Park on street.

**Admission:** Gardens free. Tours of house: adults, $1.50; children under 12, free. Group rates. Open Friday to Tuesday 11am to 4:30pm; Wednesday and Thursday 1 to 4:30pm. Closed December 1 to January 15.

**Facilities:** Restrooms, benches, drinking fountain, picnic tables, barbecues. Handicapped access good. Gazebo and patio area with kitchen may be reserved. For information call (916) 538-2497. Booklets, cards, and gifts available in house. Mistletoe party at Christmas time, flea market in spring, and annual walking tour.

**Nearby:** Oroville Chinese Temple Garden is on Broderick Street, and Kampong Gardens Nursery, with spectacular spring azalea display, is at Olive Highway and Kampong Court. Restored 1870s residence of California pioneer General John Bidwell, adjacent to campus of California State University at Chico, is a state historic monument open to the public. The entire college campus is designated as an arboretum and wildlife refuge. Many of the 135 kinds of trees and shrubs in the arboretum were planted by Bidwell more than a century ago.

# Also of Interest

**Bidwell Mansion State Historic Park**, 525 The Esplanade, Chico (916) 895-6144. Many old specimen oaks, ponderosa pines, crape myrtles, California palms, digger pines, enormous southern magnolias, and other plants around an 1868 Italianate mansion. Adjacent arboretum on California State University, Chico, campus.

**Capitol Nurseries**, three locations in Sacramento area; main nursery at 5410 Sunrise Boulevard, Citrus Heights (916) 961-9100. One of oldest all-purpose Sacramento nurseries, noted for service, variety, and quality of plants; also garden equipment, fertilizers, pots, ornaments.

**Kampong Gardens Nursery**, Olive Highway and Kam-

*Palms add vertical accents and spiky textures at Kampong Gardens*

pong Court, Oroville (916) 533- 3970. Spectacular spring azalea display, rustic setting with pond; old railroad cars and farm equipment; many unusual palms, timber bamboo, Suzuki azaleas, pleached liquidambar trees.

**King's Mums,** 20303 East Liberty Road, Clements (between Lodi and Jackson) or P.O. Box 368, Clements, 95227 (209) 759-3571. Chrysanthemums. Largely mail order through catalog; glorious blooms October through November.

**Shannon-Knox House and Gardens,** Highway 193 and Main Street, Georgetown, off Highway 49 in Sierra foothills. Historic house (not open to public), small public garden. Nearby, east of town, is a bonanza of spring bloom with old well house in field of naturalized daffodils; in nearby Georgetown gardens are old roses, some dating to Gold Rush days, at peak bloom in May.

# North Bay/Mendocino

# Old St. Hilary's

❀ Esperanza Street, Tiburon

First-time visitors to Tiburon cannot fail to notice an old, wooden church, painted white, on a grassy hillside overlooking town and the bay. Old St. Hilary's was named for the name-saint of Hilarita Reed Lyford, whose father held the Mexican grant to the land on which the church was constructed in 1886. The site was acquired in 1959 by the Belvedere-Tiburon Landmarks Society, and the four-acre wildflower garden was the society's first open-space project. In 1970 the garden was dedicated in honor of John Thomas Howell, curator emeritus of botany at the California Academy of Sciences, who observed that nowhere else in the state can "so many wonderful plants be found in so small a space."

Stone walls with built-in benches, steps, and a network of crushed stone paths are the only amenities added to what is essentially a natural preserve with varied plant habitats and incomparable views of San Francisco and the bay. The garden is best visited in mid-winter through late spring and early summer. By late summer there are few wildflowers, and the garden has taken on the parched, tan colors of grassy hills in undeveloped areas of California. This dry summer and fall phase, however, is part of the natural cycle of California plants.

In the wildflower garden at Old St. Hilary's dry rocky slopes, almost level grasslands, freshwater springs, and marshy areas support over 200 plant species, two-thirds of them native, some of them rare. Plants specially adapted to serpentine soil (derived from rock low in calcium, potassium, and phosphorus and high in magnesium and heavy metals) are found in this environment, which is toxic to or too low in nutrients to support most kinds of plants.

Visitors may see four serpentine plants, all of them rare and endangered. Tiburon paintbrush (*Castilleja neglecta*), with red-tipped yellow flowers, blooms in early spring. Marin dwarf flax (*Hesperolinon congestum*), with rose flowers, and Tiburon buckwheat (*Eriogonum caninum*), with rose-red flowers, both bloom in early summer. If you know what to look for you may see the very rare black jewelflower (*Streptanthus niger*), with dark purple flowers, found only on the southern end of the Tiburon Peninsula.

Many sedges, rushes, and ferns grow in low, wet ground and hillside seepages. The garden has twenty-four species of native grasses and many flowering annuals and perennials. Preservation of the state's flora is part of the Landmark Society's plan for this site. Thomas Howell advised: "It must not be disturbed, landscaped, planted, weeded, irrigated or walked on — just leave it to Nature."

**Getting There:** Highway 101 north of Golden Gate Bridge to Tiburon Boulevard exit. Continue into town (past sign to new church of St. Hilary's) and turn left on Beach Road, which winds uphill. Street name changes to Esperanza and street becomes narrow lane. Park in lot.

**Admission:** Free. Garden open daily all year. Church/museum open April to mid-October Wednesday and Sunday 1 to 4pm. Guided tours by appointment. Call (415) 435-1853.

**Facilities:** Benches, drinking fountain. Gifts, publications, exhibits in church/museum. Handicapped access limited.

**Nearby:** To see serpentine habitat on a grander scale, take a moderately strenuous hike up nearby Ring Mountain, a natural preserve of several hundred acres. From Old St. Hilary's go down to Tiburon Boulevard, turn right, go about two miles to Trestle Glen Road, turn right, and follow Trestle Glen to Paradise Drive. Turn left down hill. Entrance is just past Marin Country Day School. Richardson Bay Audubon Center and Sanctuary, with restored Lyford House (built in 1876), is at 376 Greenwood Beach Road, Tiburon. House tours October to May Sundays 1 to 4 pm. Sanctuary open Wednesday through Sunday 9am to 5pm. Nature trail begins on water side of Lyford House; small native plant garden beside Whittell Education Center. From Old St. Hilary's take Tiburon Boulevard toward downtown Tiburon and turn left on Greenwood Beach Road.

# Marin County Civic Center

❀ Civic Center Drive, San Rafael

The Marin County Civic Center, designed by Frank Lloyd Wright, is clearly visible from Highway 101, dramatically spanning several knolls with views of surrounding hills and San Pablo Bay. Besides attractive landscaping around the building and parking area, there are three gardens connected with the complex.

An atrium garden running through the center of the complex is a four-story, lozenge-shaped opening visible from all floors, but the planted beds are best viewed from balconies above. Elevators carry visitors to a good overview from the second floor. The raised beds below are filled with a mix of tropical and subtropical plants and others that enjoy warmth and moisture. Ornamental figs (*Ficus benjamina*), usually kept much smaller when grown as street trees, here reach their full height of twenty to thirty feet. Aralias, with big, bold leaves, are nearly as tall. Some beds are filled with English ivy, others with hostas. Plantings vary in height and texture, and all benefit from the soft light of skylights above.

On the second floor also is an outdoor terrace garden, with entry through a public cafeteria. Tables and chairs are placed around a large, round pool. A stream flowing from the pool disappears behind curved beds filled with seasonal plants and agapanthus. The water is recirculated and flows to a lower pool and fountain visible from Civic Center Drive. Fine views of oak-studded hills can be enjoyed from the cafeteria inside as well as from the terrace.

A gold, white, and blue color scheme has been followed in the plantings here, and the design motif of lozenge shapes, circles, and half-circles is apparent. Round concrete planters contain white-flowered oleanders grown as standards and blue agapanthus; yellow, orange, white, and blue annuals are planted in season. Round steppingstones and curved, raised beds with tall flax and birch trees repeat the circle motif. These plants, once established, need little water in summer.

The third garden, with access from the fourth floor at the south end of the corridor, is designed to showcase native and other drought-tolerant plants suitable for home landscapes. Among native coast live oaks, Monterey pines, and western redbuds are shrubs that persist through dry summers, including toyon, ceanothus, bearberry, rockspray cotoneaster, huckleberry manzanita, and sedums. Plants are labeled. Stone steps lead to the top of a knoll, where there is a circular patio with picnic tables and magnificent views of the surrounding area.

*Strap-shaped leaves are striking against smooth, round shapes*

**Getting There:** Highway 101 north of San Rafael. Take San Pedro Road exit north and continue to Civic Center Drive. Turn left and go about half a block to Memorial Drive. Turn left up to Civic Center, then through driveway under building to rear parking lot.

**Admission:** Open weekdays 8am to 5pm.

**Facilities:** Restrooms, drinking fountains, picnic tables, cafeteria. Handicapped access excellent except on knoll. Docent-led tours of Civic Center and gardens by appointment. Call (415) 499-6104.

**Nearby:** Farmers' market Thursdays 8am to 1pm and Sundays 9am to 2pm off Civic Center Drive in auditorium parking lot, just north of the lagoon. Marin Art and Garden Center is on Sir Francis Drake Boulevard in Ross.

# Marin Art and Garden Center

❀ Sir Francis Drake Boulevard, Ross

Only the barn, now a theater, and the Octagon House, with a library of art and garden books, remain from the turn-of-the-century ranch of the George Worn family on which the Marin Art and Garden Center was established in 1943. Though now surrounded by urban development, the wooded beauty of the ten-acre property, with small creek and many fine specimen trees, continues to give pleasure to those who use the community center facilities or come simply to enjoy the gardens.

A giant sequoia (*Sequoiadendron giganteum*) brought as a small tree from Yosemite in the 1880s by the George Worn family has a domed top characteristic of much older trees, perhaps a result of its sunny location. The tree is a living memorial to residents of Marin County who died in World War II. An unforgettable evergreen magnolia planted in a center island has a spread of over sixty-five feet. Its branches, heavy in maturity, have rooted in surrounding soil. Dozens of children could hide under the limbs of this huge tree, a memorial to George Young, husband of Frances Young, for whom the art gallery is named.

By a bridge crossing the creek, near the site of the old Worn

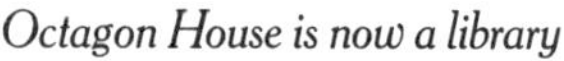

*Octagon House is now a library*

home, is a large Japanese maple planted in memory of Isabella Worn. This bridge leads to a rambling complex of low buildings housing a restaurant, shops, and offices of community organizations connected by brick walkways and small patios and gardens. Benches conveniently placed among holly trees, oaks, Japanese lace-leaf maples, a tri-color beech, and beds of annuals and perennials give these areas intimacy and charm. A large patio with raised stage under enormous oaks is used for fashion shows, luncheons, and other events.

In front of the art gallery is a tall dawn redwood (*Metasequoia glyptostroboides*), a memorial to Marin artist Alice Montague. Other memorial trees are a black oak in memory of Tiernon Berry, who planted many oaks in the area, and a golden locust in memory of Roger Sohner, an early director of the center. There is also a memory garden, maintained by the Marin Garden Club in tribute to Marin County residents.

Circular gravel terraces feature bird baths, statues, benches, and shade-loving plants under trees, and a curved loggia with vine-covered arbor looks out on a large pool with fountain. This is a popular place for weddings and other celebrations.

**Getting There:** Highway 101 to Sir Francis Drake Boulevard exit west to the village of Ross. The entrance is just past Berry Lane, on the right, near the intersection of Sir Francis Drake and Laurel Grove Avenue. Park in lot.

**Admission:** Grounds open daily. Art gallery open Monday through Thursday 11am to 4pm, Saturday and Sunday 1 to 4pm. Restaurant open Tuesday through Friday 11:30am to 2pm.

**Facilities:** Benches, restrooms, drinking fountains, art gallery, restaurant, shops, library, theater. Handicapped access excellent. Garden lectures and meetings; fall flower festival; Christmas greens sale; fashion shows; art rental. Facilities available for public use, call (415) 454-5597.

**Nearby:** Continue west on Sir Francis Drake Boulevard to Inverness and Point Reyes National Seashore, with lighthouse, reproduction of a Miwok Indian village, and good whale-watching in fall and early winter. South from Inverness on Panoramic Highway is Muir Woods, over 500 acres of redwood groves with associated plants, some labeled.

# Ira Cook House

❀ 1125 B Street, San Rafael

For an enjoyable outing, pack a picnic, gather the family, and visit the Ira Cook House and Boyd Memorial Park in San Rafael. The extensive gardens and park are a short walk from downtown San Rafael. The park and gardens, which overlook town, were once part of Maple Lawn, the Cook family estate. Given to the city in 1905 by Cook's granddaughter Louise and her husband John Franklin Boyd, the property is now a city park. The well-preserved house, built in 1879, has been the Marin Historical Society Museum since 1955.

A small, cobbled stream flows down from the highest point of the property beside a redwood-edged path. The source of the stream is a spring that fills an old reservoir built for the estate. Its water, which once quenched the thirst and filled the tubs of most of San Rafael's population, is still in use. The stone-walled reservoir is fenced, but pond plants and a small waterfall that plunges from a pipe can be seen.

Many old Japanese maple trees, for which the estate was named, are lovely in autumn when the leaves blaze with color. Magnolias, nandina, cotoneaster, holly, and clumping bamboo also have been in the garden for many years. Much of the wide lawn has been replaced with a children's playground.

There is a specimen monkey puzzle tree (*Araucaria araucana*) near the iron-gated driveway. These trees, which grow to 200 feet, often were planted on early California estates and in parks as landmark trees. Visitors may not want to picnic under the monkey puzzle tree, since large cones sometimes drop from a great height. There are picnic tables at many other places in the park.

Tall deodar cedars by the house, a cedar of Lebanon, and one of the few producing date palms in Northern California also are of interest. Camellias and hydrangeas, which line the fence along Mission Street, are cherished old plants. A few fragrant shrubs of *Daphne odora*, called winter daphne because it blooms in February and March, survive from earlier days. Many native oaks, big-leaf maples, and redwoods grow in the park and on the hillside.

John Frederick Jordan of Boston, said to be the first landscape architect in San Rafael, designed the grounds. Later, Ah Sing, a Chinese gardener, cared for the gardens for over fifty years. Perhaps he rested under the aged wisteria twining over an arbor and small stone hut beside the house. From the arbor, a walk through the front yard leads to an intricate wrought-iron gate with

*Cherished old plants frame house and border wrought-iron fence*

tall, columnar yews towering over it. The elaborate black iron fence surrounding the garden, inlaid with gold leaf, is worth a trip itself. Gardeners of today can only dream of such exquisite craftsmanship in their own backyards.

**Getting There:** Highway 101 to Fourth Street in San Rafael. Head west on Fourth Street to C Street and turn right. Go two blocks to Mission and turn right to B Street. Park on street.

**Admission:** Park and garden free; entry to museum in house by donation. Park and garden open daily 9am to 6pm; museum open Wednesday through Sunday 1 to 4pm.

**Facilities:** Restrooms, benches, picnic tables, children's playground. Handicapped access limited. Tennis courts reserved through San Rafael Parks and Recreation Department (415) 485-3333.

**Nearby:** Mt. Tamalpais State Park, a few miles southwest of San Rafael, is a 6,233-acre preserve of redwood and other coastal trees, with hiking, camping, and picnicking facilities.

# John's Rose Garden

❀ 1020 Mt. George Avenue, Napa

Tucked away in a semi-rural residential area where large oaks line the streets is a garden and nursery specializing in roses. Owner John Dallas had two reasons for planting over 500 varieties of roses on his one-and-a-half-acre lot: first, to introduce visitors to less common roses, and second, to let visitors see how to use large shrub roses, climbers, and miniature roses in the landscape.

The garden began as a personal one, then grew as years went by. After retirement from the army, Dallas taught landscaping classes for eight years at Solano Community College, then turned to tending his garden. Besides roses, there are over twenty-five trees, including native valley oaks, Japanese black pines, weeping crabapples, eucalypts, ginkgoes, liquidambars, and redwoods. A

*Roses mix contentedly with many other plants*

grove of birches with a carpet of violets beneath lends a woodland atmosphere near the house entrance.

The garden thrives with no chemical sprays. With so many other things to do John says he "just doesn't get to it" and has "no drastic problems." The roses are fed with slow-release fertilizer and are on automatic drip irrigation. Leaves and clippings are composted with wood chips, and the resulting mulch is used throughout the garden.

Among the garden's hundreds of roses are such old varieties as 'Empress Josephine' (1770), 'Maiden's Blush' (prior to 1797), 'Old Blush' (1759), and 'Celsiana' (prior to 1750). Several arbors showcase shrub and climbing roses. 'Climbing La France' and 'White Dawn' make a pleasing combination on a backyard arbor. *Rosa rubrifolia* is notable for its purplish green foliage and red hips; 'Cardinal Richelieu' and 'Sparrieshoop' are outstanding shrub roses. *Rosa rugosa* 'Rubra', a vigorous old rugosa rose with perfumed flowers, grows happily near the duck pond. 'Dortmund', with single red blooms, covers an arbor of curved slats. Benches are placed so that visitors can enjoy the fragrance of roses and views of Mt. George.

Sun-loving roses do well near a native plant area with toyon, manzanitas, California fuchsia, and flannel bush. Large shrubs interplanted effectively with roses are smoke bush, bottlebrush, crape myrtle, and purple-flowered buddleia. Hollyhocks, penstemons, and Shasta daisies along the paths add country-cottage charm. Irises, daffodils, and other bulbs start the spring blooming season. The best time to see roses in bloom is mid-April to mid-June.

**Getting There:** Highway 80 to Highway 29 through Vallejo to Napa, then north to Silverado Trail (Highway 121). Continue to Hagen Road and turn right. Go to Olive Hill Lane, turn left, then left again on Mt. George Avenue. Park on street or in driveway.

**Admission:** Free. By appointment (707) 224-8002.

**Facilities:** Benches. Handicapped access good. Annual spring open house.

**Nearby:** Napa Valley wineries, many with historic buildings and gardens, are north on Highway 29. On the way, stop in Yountville at McAllister Water Gardens, specializing in moisture-loving and pond plants.

# Napa Valley Wineries

❀ Rutherford and St. Helena

Napa Valley is famous not only for its fine wines and popular winery tours but for the wide variety of other things to do: balloon and glider rides, bicycling, golfing, horseback riding, browsing in antique and specialty shops, and dining in the valley's many restaurants, known for their use of fresh California produce, cheeses, and wines. Many wineries in Napa Valley, as elsewhere in California, are surrounded by beautiful landscapes with stunning hilltop or valley views. Just three Napa Valley wineries with historic homes and gardens — Inglenook/Napa Valley, Sutter Home, and Beringer — are described here to give a "taste" of those open to visitors.

The hundred-year-old wine cellars of Inglenook/Napa Valley Winery are on St. Helena Highway in Rutherford. The long driveway to an old yellow farmhouse is lined with maples, purple-leaf plums, and crabapples, with vineyards stretching out on either side. Sycamores and purple-leaf plums shade the parking lot. Wide brick walks lead past the farmhouse, where roses twine on porch posts and an orange tree has been bearing fruit for decades. Half wine barrels filled with colorful annuals are placed around the extensive brick courtyard shaded by a huge oak tree. Leaves of Virginia creeper covering the front of the building and rows of ornamental 'Bradford' pears across the courtyard turn scarlet-red and burgundy in autumn.

Near the winery entrance a lemon tree with navel orange branches grafted onto it produces both fruits. The broad courtyard with benches and central fountain looks out to views of vineyards and valley. Old wine caves with arched ceilings resembling the curve of a barrel are a cool respite on hot days.

Also on St. Helena Highway, in St. Helena, is Sutter Home Winery, the executive offices of which are in a magnificent restored Victorian house built in 1884. The carriage house and replica of the original water tower have been made into a bed-and-breakfast inn. Surrounding the house is a Victorian-style garden behind iron fences. Tall palm trees, often used in turn-of-the-century California gardens, and native valley oaks tower above house and garden.

Brick walks separate raised beds of fragrant old roses underplanted with annuals and perennials that spill over rock walls and scent the air. This charming garden also has a lacy Victorian gazebo, small lawns, and a fountain frequented by birds.

The steep-roofed, stone mansion of Beringer Vineyards, built in 1883, is on Main Street in St. Helena. Rooms in the mansion today are used for offices, wine tasting, and gift shop. Caves dug into the hillside are still used to store wines. The landscape features sweeping lawns with oaks, elms, redwoods, Japanese maples, and liquidambar trees. Large oleanders and urns filled with annuals give summer color. Curved beds by the house are planted with nandina, agapanthus, and boxwood hedges. Palms and the pendulous branches of deodar cedars add contrasting textures and shapes. A plaque at the base of an old oak tree, placed by the National Association of Arborists, notes that the tree was living at the time of the signing of the U.S. Constitution.

Wide stone terraces with broad steps surround the Beringer mansion. Low stone walls and sunny flower beds accent three peaked-roof gazebos with comfortable benches. A fountain, with figures designed by San Francisco sculptor Ruth Asawa, commemorates the 150th anniversary of the planting of the first grape vine in the Napa Valley by George Yount. The eight-foot bronze sculpture also depicts Jacob and Frederick Beringer, German immigrants and vintners who founded the winery in 1876.

**Getting There:** Highway 80 to Highway 29 in Vallejo north past Napa to Rutherford and St. Helena. Inglenook is at 1991 St. Helena Highway in Rutherford; Sutter Home is at 277 St. Helena Highway in St. Helena; Beringer is at 2000 Main Street in St. Helena. Park in lots.

**Admission:** Free. Inglenook is open daily 10am to 5 pm; Sutter Home is open daily 10am to 4:30pm; Beringer is open daily 10am to 5pm. All are closed major holidays.

**Facilities:** All have benches and restrooms, wine tasting and sales rooms, good handicapped access. Winery tours at Inglenook (10:30am to 4pm) and Beringer (9:30am to 4pm); Sutter Home has no winery tours, but offers garden tours Friday through Sunday 11am, 1 and 2pm. Inglenook has library for wine scholars and museum of wine-related artifacts. Sutter Home has bed-and-breakfast inn with rooms opening to garden. For information: Inglenook (707) 963-3362; Sutter Home (707) 963-3104; Beringer (707) 963-7115.

**Nearby:** Silverado Museum, with mementos of the life and work of Robert Louis Stevenson, is in St. Helena, where the author lived for a short time. North on Highway 29 is Calistoga, popular for hot springs, geysers, mud baths, and balloon and glider rides. McAllister Water Gardens is south on Highway 29 in Yountville. The restored home and gardens of General Mariano Guadalupe Vallejo are on West Third Street in Sonoma.

# Garden Valley Ranch

❀ 498 Pepper Road, Petaluma

At Ray Reddell's sunny, level, seven-acre ranch three miles north of Petaluma thousands of roses are cultivated for the cut-flower market in San Francisco and throughout the country. With a hundred-year-old Victorian summer house, complete with kitchen, and a lawn large enough to accommodate tents or canopies, the site is also used for weddings and garden parties.

To the west of the summer house is a one-acre fragrant garden where plants are grown for their perfume and for blending pot-pourri. To the east are 4,000 rose bushes in double rows with grassy corridors between, good for enjoying close-up views of the flowers. A fragrant white rose, 'Sheer Bliss', is just one of many roses planted in blocks of a single color.

White lattice arches beside the summer house lead to a charming arbor draped with wisteria and jasmine. Gravel paths between beds of irises, lavender, rosemary, thyme, and other scented herbs take visitors to a sunny brick patio with a round brick pool and fountain. Raised beds at each end of the cross-shaped patio are filled with scented roses interplanted with mints, sages, basil, oregano, and other plants fragrant in foliage or flower. Yarrow, jasmine, pinks, and a mix of seasonally changing flowers add to the pleasant aroma. Bees and hummingbirds float from one heady-scented plant to another. A fence and trees give this part of the garden a sense of enclosure.

In a secluded area behind the fragrant garden a woodland of willows, twisted and leaning beside a trickling brook, gives a feeling of wildness. Birches border a shady area where mosses, violets, peonies, and camellias are sheltered by rows of Lombardy poplars. From the fragrant garden gravel paths lead back to the summer house and a tree-shaded bench looking over the lush lawn, across the colorful roses and old farm buildings, then out to grassy hills. Chimes ring in the breeze, which brings with it mingled scents of herbs and roses.

**Getting There:** Highway 101 north of Petaluma; take Old Redwood Highway/Penngrove exit west. Continue west to Stony Point Road, turn right, go to Pepper Road, and turn left. Park in lot.

**Admission:** Free. Gardens open daily 10am to 5pm. Nursery open Thursday through Sunday 10am to 4pm.

**Facilities:** Restrooms, benches, drinking fountain. Handicapped access excellent. Summer house and 5,000-square-foot lawn available for weddings and receptions. Call (707) 795-0919.

# Great Petaluma Desert Nursery

❀ 5010 Bodega Avenue, Petaluma

In dairy country northwest of Petaluma Jerry and Eiko Wright have established a cactus and succulent nursery behind their white stucco house. A huge century plant and a fourteen-foot-tall, multi-stem organ pipe cactus (*Lemaireocereus marginatus*) beside the house's arched entryway show how attractive these striking plants can be in a home landscape.

The nursery is described as a collector's mecca because of the unusual plants offered. In the greenhouse is a ten-year-old, leaf-bearing rhodocactus (*Pereskia sacharosa*), which resembles a rambling rose. Wright has been growing it for almost ten years; if he didn't prune it, it would be a small tree.

Another unusual plant, from Mexico, is the slow-growing

*Cacti are living sculptures in a desert landscape*

*Zamia pumila (Z. furfuracea)*, called Florida arrowroot or Seminole bread because of the starchy sago produced in the roots. This palm-like plant grows outdoors in mild climates or in greenhouses where winters are cool. The succulent *Didierea trollii*, from Madagascar, has thin, needle-like spines and stems that grow in a strange, zig-zag pattern, straight up for a short distance, then turning ninety degrees, straight again, then taking off at another ninety-degree angle. The nursery also is known for a large selection of Madagascar palms, unusual plants with spiny trunks.

A large new greenhouse is filled with hundreds of tall specimen cacti and succulents for sale in containers or bare-root, ready for planting. The nursery offers about as many succulents as cacti. Also offered are good selections of bromeliads and epiphytic tillandsias, usually grown without soil on slabs of bark or wood.

Comfortable benches overlook a demonstration garden landscaped in western desert style. Cacti — round, low, and spiny or tall, tree-like, and thorny — are planted among volcanic rocks on gravelly soil. Neat gravel paths lead to small propagating greenhouses and raised wood-frame beds with more mature cacti and succulents. Two large new greenhouses will soon be added.

**Getting There:** Highway 101 to Petaluma; take Washington Street/Bodega Avenue exit west through town on Bodega Avenue to nursery. Park in driveway.

**Admission:** Open Friday through Sunday 10am to 5pm; Monday through Thursday by appointment. Call (707) 778-8278.

**Facilities:** Benches, drinking fountain. Handicapped access good.

**Nearby:** Another cacti and succulent nursery in Petaluma is A Sticky Business, on Liberty Road.

# A Sticky Business

❀ 110 Liberty Road, Petaluma

Down a gravel lane and through a gated fence that keeps out vagrant sheep is a thriving cactus and succulent nursery with more than 100,000 plants. Old wooden buildings, renovated for use in propagation, are nearly hidden by the new greenhouses of an expanding business started by Allan Leroy in 1979.

A building that once housed chickens is now filled with hundreds of small pots of tiny succulents. Separated by fences, steps, and weathered wood gates, greenhouses on several levels are connected by a labyrinth of paths. Dish gardens, especially popular as gifts, usually are available or will be planted to special order.

On greenhouse benches and outside in pots and tubs are thousands of agaves, some so hardy they can be grown in Alaska.

*Palm-like succulents with spiny trunks are known as Madagascar palms*

There are also many rosette-forming dudleyas, succulents good in coastal climates, and numerous echeverias, with fleshy, crinkled leaves, pastel green shading into pink and violet, their flower stalks nodding above the plant. Blue-candle cactus (*Myrtillocactus geometrizans*) and tall, five-sided fence-post or organ pipe cactus (*Lemaireocereus marginatus*) are planted like a forest. Used for hedges in Mexico, these cacti also grow well in pots for house and patio. Taking root wherever opportunity presents is *Kalanchoe daigremontiana*, called devil's backbone or mother of thousands, the leaves of which drop when mature, producing new plantlets.

Elegant and unusual, *Aloe polyphylla* grows in big, round tubs. Native to Lesotho in South Africa, these succulents grow in chilly temperatures at altitudes of up to 9,000 feet. Their plump leaves are meticulous, tightly formed, green spirals. The plants are being nurtured to produce seeds for propagation.

Over one hundred varieties of sempervivums include many of European origin, and several varieties of hawthorias are offered, some quite rare. Leroy recommends cow's horn euphorbia (*Euphorbia grandicornis*); called the cactus of Africa, it's really a spiny succulent. The twisted, flat forms of these plants, ten to fifteen feet at maturity, are best grown indoors.

Leroy mentions the popular names of well-known varieties he offers for sale— hedge-hog, old lady, old man with a beard, old man of the mountain, fence-post, hen and chickens. These plants, and all others in the nursery, also are labeled with scientific names.

Greenhouse doors and vents are opened for air circulation, an important element for success with cacti and succulents, besides sunshine and well-drained, gritty soil. Hummingbirds especially like aloe, gasteria, and echeveria blossoms. They zoom in and out of greenhouses in their quest for nectar.

Like a man proud of his family, Leroy shows off the thousands of plants in neat rows. "I don't have to sell them," he says. "It's like a spider getting you in its web. Once you see them, you're sold."

**Getting There:** Highway 101 north of Petaluma; take Highway 116 exit west; go 1.5 miles and turn left on Stony Point Road, continue to Pepper Road, turn right and go to Liberty Road. Gravel lane leads to farm gate with sign. Close gate behind you, drive back to nursery, and park between greenhouses.

**Admission:** Open Saturday and Sunday 10am to 5pm, weekdays by appointment. Call (707) 795-3185.

**Facilities:** Restroom. Handicapped access limited.

**Nearby:** Garden Valley Ranch, which grows cut flowers for San Francisco and nationwide markets, and the Great Petaluma Desert Nursery, offering many unusual cacti and succulents, are both in Petaluma.

# Iron Horse Vineyards

❀ 9786 Ross Station Road, Sebastopol

When Barry and Audrey Sterling set out to restore Iron Horse Ranch and Vineyards outside Sebastopol in 1976, they brought Continental traditions of food, wine, and entertainment to the neglected Victorian house and 300 acres of surrounding land. Their years in San Francisco, Southern California, England, and France gave the couple an eclectic perspective.

Audrey supervised restoration of the house while Barry took charge of the vineyards; they tackled the garden together. First the tangled, overgrown hillside and ten-acre garden had to be cleared. As they opened spaces, remnants of an earlier garden — terraces, walls, and a spring — were discovered under the jungle of poison oak and blackberry vines. After clearing, planting of the new garden began, a process that continues today.

The never-ending flower show begins in early spring with over 30,000 daffodils. Tulips, cyclamens, primroses, lilies, and other bulbs follow. Flowering trees grown partly for indoor arrangements begin with the deciduous magnolias (tulip trees), then flowering quince, dogwood, laurel, lilac, flowering pear, crabapple, and cherry. Wisteria on arbors and porch pillars adds to the display.

The focal point of a favorite patio for summer lunches is an aged, mossy plumcot tree developed by Luther Burbank, whose Sebastopol growing fields are a few miles away. Windows of the old house look out on a hillside view of rhododendrons, azaleas, camellias, foxgloves, columbines, irises, and delphiniums. These and other plants bloom along paths and in terraced beds beneath oaks, bay laurels, and buckeyes.

An allée of London plane trees was planted along stone walls built by the family and vineyard workers. Other stone-walled, raised beds provide ideal drainage for vegetables and cut flowers. Herbs grown in half barrels from the winery are used in the kitchen all summer or dried for later use. Fresh vegetables and fruits are the basis for harvest lunches in late summer and fall.

Baskets of petunias, impatiens, and begonias hang from porches and decorate tables and patios. Lilies, blooming throughout spring and summer, are splashes of color in pots and tubs; they are Barry's favorites, and he plants new ones every year.

Summer is peak blooming time for over 200 roses, including heirloom varieties. The billowing pink flowers of 'Cécile Brunner' adorn a fence, and the pink and red flowers of others are echoed in phlox, hollyhocks, and crape myrtle. A nineteenth-century arbor is covered with the deliciously fragrant old Bourbon rose 'Honorine de Brabant'.

Fall color blazes in red pyracantha berries. Acres of grape leaves turn tawny gold, and the changing leaves of liquidambar, ginkgo, fruit, and poplar trees add to autumn's brilliance. The garden is a continuing pageant.

**Getting There:** Highway 101 north of Petaluma; exit on Highway 116 west through Sebastopol. About 2.5 miles past the intersection with Guerneville Road, turn left on Ross Station Road and follow it to the end. Turn right to winery parking lot.

**Admission:** Free. Gardens open by appointment only, in season. Winetasting and winery tours by appointment, usually at 10am and 3pm daily, including weekends, but call (707) 887-1507 before coming.

**Facilities:** Benches in garden. Restrooms, wine and gifts for sale at winery. Handicapped access generally good, but some parts of garden inaccessible by wheelchair.

**Nearby:** Luther Burbank home and gardens are a few miles away in Santa Rosa.

# Miniature Plant Kingdom

❀ 4125 Harrison Grade Road, Sebastopol

In a semi-rural setting where houses are separated by several acres is a nursery that specializes in miniature roses and plants used for bonsai. There are 50,000 miniature roses in greenhouses and about one-half acre of roses planted beside the driveway. Outstanding are 'Star Twinkle', with pointed petals of clear orange-red, and 'Yellow Doll', with soft, buttery yellow blossoms. Thousands of miniature roses on tables in two large greenhouses afford a wide choice, whether purchased in containers for patio and porch or in pots for planting in the ground. The flowers of miniature roses come in many colors, and all are as perfectly formed as larger roses but so tiny that they fit comfortably in a demitasse cup. Their beautifully formed foliage is as exquisite as the flowers.

Unusual and varied bonsai starts include numerous specimens from the Orient: a Korean lilac only four inches high with tiny, fragrant flowers or a dwarf myrtle with leaves one-eighth inch wide and one-half inch long. Elms are favorite trees for bonsai treatment, and the Japanese hokkaido elm, which grows only eighteen inches high in ten years, is choice. Other trees, grown in lovely Japanese pots, are crabapples, ginkgoes, cypresses, and groves of miniature beeches.

*Miniature railroad is in scale with dwarf plants*

Japanese hinoki cypress is a superb tree for bonsai because it grows very slowly, attaining less than two feet in height in a decade. Slow-growing varieties of Japanese cedar, spruce, pine, and juniper also are ideal for container, dish, and rock gardens, as well as bonsai. Oaks, elms, and pines are trained into picturesque shapes to achieve an ancient appearance in a short time. Some slow-growing shrubs that make good bonsai subjects are dwarf podocarpus, pyracantha, azalea, and prostrate cotoneaster.

Ornamental grasses are often planted as accents beside a bonsai tree or grown in containers by themselves. Unusual offerings at this nursery are corkscrew rush, with tubular, twisted stems; dwarf black mondo grass, only six inches high; and many miniature bamboos.

**Getting There:** Highway 101 north of Petaluma; take Highway 116 exit west and continue through Sebastopol to Graton Road. Turn left, go to Tanuda Road, turn right, then turn right on DuPont Road, and very shortly turn left on Harrison Grade Road. Watch for nursery sign. Gravel drive leads back to nursery. Park in lot.

**Admission:** Open Thursday through Sunday 9am to 4pm; Monday and Tuesday by appointment. Call (707) 874-2233.

**Facilities:** Restrooms. Handicapped access good.

**Nearby:** Manning's Heather Farm and Sonoma Horticultural Nursery are also in Sebastopol, as is Iron Horse Vineyards, with garden of year-round interest.

# Sonoma Horticultural Nursery

❀ 3970 Azalea Avenue, Sebastopol

Rhododendrons and azaleas are the specialty here, but the nursery also offers companion plants that do well in the same conditions — filtered light and well-drained soil high in organic matter. Over 300 azaleas and about an equal number of rhododendrons are planted in a shady woodland. April is the best month to enjoy the display of flowering plants surrounding a pond and under a canopy of oaks, pines, Japanese maples, and redwoods. Winding paths with footbridges over low places between chest-high rhododendrons and azaleas give visitors the feeling of being part of this show of living color.

A plank bridge spanning a creek leads to a clearing with display garden. In this sunny space are a grove of birches, willows, fruit trees, eastern and western redbuds, and lombardy poplars in a row along the creek bank. Several varieties of dogwood do well in dappled light under taller trees. Low woodland plants — ferns, hostas, sorrels, and columbines — grow in rich humus along with azaleas and rhododendrons.

A path circles the pond, which is enjoyed by an assortment of ducks. This lovely landscaped area with picnic tables has a wonderful view of rhododendrons and azaleas reflected in the pond. Flowering cherries and crabapples along the north bank add to the beauty in spring. At the end of the pond is an area of deciduous Exbury azaleas, noted for their bright, almost glowing flower colors.

Also offered are tropical vireya rhododendrons, which prefer greenhouse conditions during cold months; Japanese miniature azaleas, excellent for rock gardens and containers; and Sonoma hybrid and Sonoma dwarf azaleas, suitable for borders or ground cover. Companion plants include many ornamental Japanese maples, Japanese katsura trees (*Cercidiphyllum japonicum*), clematis, daphnes, and dove trees (*Davidia involucrata*), with bracts said to resemble white doves resting on the branches.

For a summer conversation starter *Gunnera chilensis* is outstanding; the nursery's specimen grows at one end of the pond where the roots stay moist, a necessary condition for good growth. This dramatic perennial with giant leaves dies back in winter except in very mild areas. New leaves from four to eight feet long rise from the center each spring, attaining full maturity in summer. Flowers resembling corncobs grow near the roots, and tiny red fruits follow. The nursery offers these plants in one- and five-gallon cans.

Empress trees, magnolias, dawn redwoods, dwarf heathers and heaths, and Japanese irises, good for edges of ponds and streams, are some of the plants that round out the wide selection in this woodland nursery.

**Getting There:** Highway 101 north of Petaluma; take Highway 116 exit west to Hessel Road and turn left. Follow Hessel, bearing right where it meets Turner Road, then continue to McFarlane Road, turn left, then right on Azalea Avenue. Park in lot.

**Admission:** Open daily March through May 9am to 5pm; closed Tuesdays and Wednesdays rest of year, except by appointment. Call (707) 823-6832.

**Facilities:** Picnic tables, benches, brochures. Handicapped access limited.

**Nearby:** Manning's Heather Farm, Lone Pine Gardens, and Bamboo Sorcery are three special nurseries in Sebastopol. Iron Horse Vineyards, with fine garden, is also in Sebastopol.

# Manning's Heather Farm

❀ 12450 Fiori Lane, Sebastopol

Follow country roads lined with redwoods, coast live oaks, madrones, and pines to a one-acre nursery specializing in Australian and New Zealand tea trees (*Leptospermum*). Thirty-five to forty species and varieties of these evergreen shrubs and small trees are available here, the largest selection in the local nursery trade.

The plants came to be known as tea trees because leaves were brewed in the 1700s to prevent scurvy among crews of sailing ships. Characterized by neat, small, leaves and tiny, jewel-like flowers that cover the plants, leptospermums are widely used in drought-tolerant landscapes. Flower colors range from white or rose-pink to deep maroon-red. Some varieties have purplish bronze leaves and reddish stems.

A favorite at the nursery is 'Manning's Choice' (a cultivated variety of *Leptospermum rotundifolia*), up to eight feet tall, with neat, round leaves. Compact plants of *Leptospermum nanum* grow only three feet high and have a tiered, layered look as they mature, with pink flowers, darker in the center. Groundcovering plants, some only a foot high and spreading four or five feet wide, also are available. Leptospermums not only are drought-tolerant but

*Dwarf conifers and leptospermums embrace lichen-covered rocks*

typically are not bothered by deer. Most bloom from February to July and are excellent for hedges, as single shrubs or trees, and in rock gardens.

The nursery originally was known for true heathers (*Calluna*) and heaths (*Erica*) and still offers a good selection of these plants. These are also evergreen shrubs with fine, needle-like or small leaves. Heathers have spikes of white, pink, lavender, or purple flowers, and heaths have clusters of bell-shaped or tubular white, pink, rosy red, or purple flowers. Both are excellent shrubs, ground covers, or rock garden plants.

Manning's also has a small demonstration rock garden, which displays leptospermums, heaths, heathers, and conifers, including a seventeen-year-old dwarf Alberta spruce, very slow growing and now only about three feet high. A rock rose (*Cistus* 'Sunset'), a drought-tolerant shrub unpalatable to deer, is only two and one-half feet tall. Also generally in stock are dwarf pines and daphnes, as well as many kinds of Japanese maples, offered for sale only after they have adjusted to the local climate.

Ferns, camellias, and other shade plants grow under redwoods along a ravine. A man-made lake, filled from a hillside spring, is used to water plants. Even in drought years Manning's has water for irrigating plants, but it is used wisely. Staff are happy to recommend water-conserving plants to visitors.

**Getting There:** Highway 101 north of Petaluma to Highway 116 exit west to Sebastopol. Go through town to Highway 12 (Bodega Highway) west and continue five miles to Jonive Road. Turn right, go 1.5 miles to Fiori Lane, turn left, and continue one-half mile to nursery. Park in front.

**Admission:** Open Thursday through Sunday 9am to 4pm February through November.

**Facilities:** Restroom, benches, drinking fountain. Handicapped access limited.

**Nearby:** Iron Horse Vineyards and Sonoma Horticultural Nursery, both in Sebastopol, are well worth a visit.

# Western Hills Nursery

❀ 16250 Coleman Valley Road, Occidental

When the late Lester Hawkins, noted landscape designer, and his partner, plantsman Marshall Olbrich, started a garden in 1959 in the hills above Occidental it was to be their personal garden. But as they began raising plants for landscaping jobs, and unusual and rare plants were added, the need for a retail nursery became obvious. Now the three-acre garden and nursery displays and sells many plants not commonly found in the trade, including an exceptional collection of perennials, rock garden plants, and California natives. Most plants in the display garden are labeled, and those that are not can be identified by knowledgeable staff.

Winding gravel paths and rich plantings give the garden a feeling of being much larger than it is. A stroll through the garden

*Display garden is a plant lover's feast*

is a plant lover's feast. The Western Hills experience is Zen-like — chimes ring in the breeze, birds flit everywhere, water ripples, and one walks on, finding surprises at every turn.

A plump cat lolls domestically in the path, but wildness seems to be just outside the fence, beyond the tall bentwood arches that define the eastern edge of the garden. Deer may come poking around at dusk, and surely raccoons and possums waddle to the small pond after dark. Leaves of quaking aspen rustle, spinning in the sun. A visitor seated on a wood bench near a flowering cock-spur coral tree is startled by a white-barked eucalyptus trunk — a slash of white, like an artist's bold brush stroke against the blue sky. Native buckeye, cotoneaster, oaks, and currants thrive in the sun. Many sages — the deepest blue-violet blossoms are those of the South American *Salvia guaranitica* — are a rich contrast to blood-red Mexican cosmos.

Little footbridges, each one different, cross a graveled stream and lead to new vistas: a sunny slope of rock garden plants, rare and unusual alpines, shade and woodland plants. Hummingbirds buzz in and out, hawks circle overhead, and a hint of ocean air from Bodega Bay floats over the ridge. It is a magical place.

**Getting There:** Highway 101 north of Petaluma; take Highway 116 exit west to Highway 12 (Bodega Road). Continue to crossroads before Freestone, bear right onto Bohemian Highway to Occidental. Turn left onto Coleman Valley Road and go uphill about a mile. Park in front.

**Admission:** Open Wednesday through Sunday 10am to 5pm.

**Facilities:** Restrooms, benches. Handicapped access limited in garden. Call (707) 874-3731.

**Nearby:** The town of Occidental is known for its authentic Italian restaurants. Interesting shops are here, too, and Russian River resorts and beaches are only a short distance away. Wishing Well Nursery, with antique shop, is on Bohemian Highway in Freestone. Sonoma Coast State Beach, with thirteen miles of scenic shoreline, is on Highway 1 near Bodega Bay.

# Luther Burbank Gardens

❀ Santa Rosa Avenue, Santa Rosa

Surrounding land is covered with buildings in downtown Santa Rosa, but almost half of the four-acre garden where plant breeder Luther Burbank conducted his experiments from 1875 until his death in 1926 has been preserved as a national and state historic landmark. The 1884 Victorian cottage, carriage house, greenhouse, and part of the gardens were given to the city in 1977.

Native oaks, fruit trees, and a huge, fragrant cedar of Lebanon — under which Burbank is buried — mask traffic noise on Santa Rosa Avenue. Several of the more than 800 plants Burbank introduced are represented here, including the Shasta daisy, white-flowered agapanthus, and a tall, yellow-flowered red-hot poker (*Kniphofia uvaria* 'Tower of Gold').

A plant unusual in Burbank's time, brought to him from China, twines around a post of the garden shelter. Known then as climbing plum, it is the now familiar kiwi (*Actinidia chinensis*).

Burbank was criticized in his day for not keeping what botanists consider scientific records, and he was derided for ideas such as the spineless cactus he developed, a large, spreading example of which grows near the house off Tupper Street. But his dedication and hard work enabled him to contribute many new fruits, vegetables, and flowers at a time when California's horticultural and agricultural markets were expanding rapidly. In the side yard is a plumcot he produced from a cross of apricot and plum. In early summer you may see its beautiful orange-gold and purple fruit. Burbank also developed the Santa Rosa plum, still the most important commercial and home-grown variety.

In the brick courtyard between the cottage and carriage house is a Camperdown elm that Burbank grafted high up on another elm so that the weeping branches would form a tent of leaves high enough to walk under. His original greenhouse is used to display plants and some of his tools. A fountain, waterfall, and pool are nearby.

Past the carriage house, look for a rare evergreen Himalayan dogwood leaning over the fence near the rose garden. Next to the dogwood is a large 'Paradox' walnut, a result of Burbank's work with native California nut trees. These trees are grown for their beautiful wood rather than their nuts; paneling in the Burbank home is 'Paradox' walnut.

The small, unpretentious home reflects Burbank's own tastes and those of his loving widow, who, for many years after his death, cared for the house and garden and the memorabilia of her hus-

*Burbank's greenhouse and white-flowered agapanthus*

band's life work in trust for the enjoyment of future generations. Most of Burbank's life was spent in solitary work with plants, but his accomplishments were widely publicized. Many visitors came, including Henry Ford, Thomas Edison, and other creative and successful people of the time. Burbank, often called the Plant Wizard, was a self-made man and inventor too.

**Getting There:** Highway 101 to Santa Rosa; take downtown exit east to Santa Rosa Avenue, turn right, and go three blocks to Sonoma Avenue. Park on street or in municipal lots.

**Admission:** Adults, $1; children under 12 with adults, free. No charge to tour garden only. Garden open all year. Home open early April to mid-October Wednesday through Sunday 10am to 3:30pm. Docent-guided tours on half hour. Group tours in season by appointment. Call (707) 576-5115.

**Facilities:** Restroom, benches, drinking fountain. Handicapped access good. Small museum, gift shop, list of plants in garden, books, and brochures available in carriage house.

**Nearby:** Robert Ripley ("Believe It Or Not") Museum in the Church of One Tree (constructed entirely of wood from one redwood tree) is across Sonoma Street, adjoining the city park. South on Highway 12 are Wildwood Farm Nursery on Sonoma Highway in Kenwood and the historic home and garden of General Mariano Guadalupe Vallejo in Sonoma. Jack London State Historic Park is near Glen Ellen.

# Kyoto Koi & Garden Center

❀ 2783 Guerneville Road, Santa Rosa

Colorful banners on tall poles in the parking lot signify the presence of something unusual here. The entrance to this special nursery, with adjacent Japanese-style rock and water garden, is a curved bridge over a stream alive with sinuous koi fish. Visitors stop to admire the varied colors, markings, and sizes of these elegant carp, favored by collectors for their beauty and longevity.

Soft music permeates the lofty buildings. Bonsai plants — some old, others starter size — fill tables and slatted benches. One section of the building is devoted to bonsai tools, equipment, and pots, including rough, hand-made ones. Beside wide windows bonsai master Hiroshi Suzuki grooms and shapes plants, which can be custom ordered. Visitors watch him repotting, pruning, and wiring bonsai plants.

Wide aisles and spacious, airy rooms afford comfortable browsing among labeled plants. Besides bonsai, many varieties of Japanese maples and bamboos are offered. There is also a mixed selection of perennials, shrubs, and trees. Koi are displayed in fish tanks. The garden center sells everything needed to keep them and gives advice about fish care and pool construction.

*Rocks are strong element of Japanese garden design*

In the outdoor plant area, where the stream emerges from under the building, extraordinary bonsai plants are displayed against a wall. Redwood tables are filled with hundreds of bonsai plants — camellias, fruiting crabapples, ancient-looking pines, junipers, and miniature groves of trees.

The stream continues into the Japanese garden, where it forms a pond fed by waterfalls that cascade from mountain-like rocks. Gravel paths accented by massive stone lanterns and large rocks lead to secluded areas with benches under maples, birches, pines, and alders. Tall clumps of bamboo, pruned pine trees — some with branches weighted with rocks to shape their growth — corkscrew willows, dogwoods, and lace-leaf Japanese maples are planted in beds and mounds around the pond and stream. A bridge of stone slabs and a feathery hedge of tall bamboo add interest to the landscape.

**Getting There:** Highway 101 to Santa Rosa; take Guerneville Road exit west. Park in lot.

**Admission:** Free. Open daily 9am to 5:30pm.

**Facilities:** Benches, restrooms. Handicapped access excellent in nursery and outdoor plant area, but paths in Japanese garden are mostly gravel. Custom pruning and potting of bonsai can be arranged. Call (707) 575-9223.

**Nearby:** Neon Palm Nursery, with many unusual palms, is on Sebastopol Road in Santa Rosa. Wildwood Farm Nursery, with many native plants, has two locations, one on Sonoma Highway in Kenwood, the other on Glen Ellen Grist Mill Road in Glen Ellen.

# Empire Nursery

❀ 3747 Guerneville Road, Santa Rosa

In a lovely rural setting about five miles west of Santa Rosa is a fine nursery with display gardens covering about one-third of the three-acre site. In the nursery, in addition to the usual stock, are many varieties of pelargoniums and geraniums. Bamboos, Japanese maples, and hanging baskets of flowers are other specialties.

A path from the nursery leads to a secluded area with wooden benches from which to enjoy the sounds of birds and the rustling of bamboo. Sunlight through birch trees creates moving shadows on the path. Large rocks, a footbridge over a small stream, and low bamboo fences around beds and mounds with shade plants add to the meditative mood.

Another path leads to a wood and bamboo pavilion built

*Oriental-style bridge zig-zags across small stream*

partially over the stream and a pond enjoyed by koi fish and ducks. Benches in the pavilion look out on a waterfall and moisture-loving plants, including waterlilies, rushes, and Japanese irises. Stone lanterns provide accents, and Japanese curtains on a bamboo pole across the entry flutter in the breeze.

Unusual plants along the path further on include an espaliered Hollywood juniper pruned as a bonsai, weeping deodar cedars, and tri-color dogwoods. Pathside beds are filled with many shrubs, trees, bamboos, and roses. Nearby is a Japanese maple house with an orange-red dragon gate. A sign overhead is translated, "You are always welcome here." Shade cloth protects many Japanese maples, including 'Butterfly', 'Crimson Queen', and 'Ever-Red Laceleaf'. Next to the maple house is a patio garden under an old, spreading oak with picnic tables and benches. A screened pen holds chickens, doves, and pheasants. Nearby is a topiary figure of a kangaroo.

A building with a mission-style facade and arched entrance houses plants that need protection from sun, including ferns, fuchsias, rhododendrons, dogwoods, camellias, and azaleas. Golden bamboo, one of many bamboos offered at the nursery, makes an airy wall along the back fence.

**Getting There:** Highway 101 to Santa Rosa. Take Guerneville Road exit west and go about five miles to nursery. Park in lot.

**Admission:** Open daily 9am to 5:30pm (5pm in winter).

**Facilities:** Restrooms, picnic tables, benches. Handicapped access good. For information call (707) 546-1113.

**Nearby:** Urban Tree Farm is on Old Redwood Highway. California Flora Nursery, specializing in native and Mediterranean-climate plants, is just north of Santa Rosa at Somers and D streets in Fulton.

# Korbel Winery

❀ 13250 River Road, Guerneville

Northwest of Santa Rosa, River Road winds past vineyards and apple orchards, then parallels the Russian River, bordered by oaks and redwoods. Boat rentals and campgrounds dot the bank. Across a bridge and around a curve, a large clearing opens up. The old brick buildings of Korbel Champagne Cellars and restored 1870s home of the Korbel family dominate the hill above the river valley.

Terraced flower beds in the parking area give a taste of the larger garden above. Restoration of the home landscape began in 1979 when an English cottage-style garden was established on slopes around the house. The only level area is a velvety lawn, ringed with large redwoods, behind the house. Picket fences, latticed porch, and the white-painted house are accented with colorful perennials and cascading roses for which the Korbel garden is especially known.

A mixture of annuals and perennials in the hillside beds assures that as flowers fade, others come into bloom. The steep path beside the driveway is lined with hydrangeas (the fragrant oak-leaf *Hydrangea quercifolia* is unusual), over twenty kinds of hostas in shady borders, and yellow-flowered Chinese lantern (*Abutilon*), an evergreen, viny shrub with drooping, bell-like flowers. Scented geraniums and sea holly, with thistle-like amethyst flowers, stand out among smaller plants.

Many South African bulbs and irises bloom early, followed by foxgloves, azaleas, fuchsias, rhododendrons, phlox, and spicy-scented pinks as spring flows into summer.

Late May is peak blooming time for 250 kinds of roses, including many old, heritage varieties. Notable are 'Perle d'Or', with pink-gold blooms, and 'Souvenir de la Malmaison', pink and fragrant, near the gazebo. Silvery lavender 'Sterling Silver' and a yellow-flowered hybrid tea, 'King's Ransom', are lovely, more recent roses. 'Belle of Portugal', with huge pink flowers, called grandmother's hat (when grandmothers wore them), is glorious on the hill.

Medicinal and culinary herbs fill beds near the house, and an area for attracting butterflies has artemisia, verbena, lavender, cosmos, and love-lies-bleeding (*Amaranthus caudatus*), an annual used in Victorian gardens, with drooping, red flowers.

Between paths circling slopes below the house is a shady garden, with begonias, hostas, impatiens, astilbes, columbines, lilies, and other plants that grow well under redwoods. A sunny area with

*Water and flowering plants attract birds and butterflies*

pool and fountain features 'Fragrant Cloud' roses, with pinkish red to purplish blooms, black-eyed Susan, balloon flowers, Mexican marigolds, euphorbias, and red-flowered cannas.

An evergreen shrub used in old gardens, called cashmere bouquet (*Clerodendrum bungei*) because of its strongly scented flowers, grows near the redwoods. Large pink- and white-flowered oleanders grow by the path leading to a grassy picnic area.

**Getting There:** Highway 101 north of Santa Rosa; take River Road exit west and go about 12.5 miles. Winery is about three miles east of Guerneville. Park in lot.

**Admission:** Free. Garden open May to October Tuesday through Sunday 10am to 4pm. Free tours hourly. Winery open daily; May through September: tours 9:45am to 3:45pm, wine tasting 9am to 5pm, wine shop 9am to 5:30pm; October through April: tours 10am to 3pm, tasting 9am to 4:30pm, wine shop 9am to 5pm. For group tours, call (707) 887-2294.

**Facilities:** Restrooms, picnic grounds, shops, museum, wine tasting. Handicapped access limited in garden.

**Nearby:** Boat rentals and private campgrounds are along Russian River. Armstrong Redwoods State Reserve and Austin Creek State Recreation Area with campsites and hiking are a few miles north, outside Guerneville, which has swimming beaches along river, restaurants, and shops in rustic redwood setting. North on Highway 1 are Fort Ross State Historic Park and Kruse Rhododendron Reserve, a natural garden of native rhododendrons among redwood trees.

# Fetzer's Valley Oaks

❀ Highway 175, Hopland

In the lush Sanel Valley, about fifty miles north of Santa Rosa, a bio-intensive garden is being developed among 200-year-old oak trees at Fetzer Vineyards' Valley Oaks Food and Wine Center.

The ranch, first settled about the time of the Gold Rush, was once devoted to growing hops for use in brewing beer. Now the barns, hop-drying sheds, and other old farm buildings have been transformed into a country inn, offices, conference center, meeting rooms, and food and wine center. Some of the ranchland has been turned into an organic garden.

Head gardener Michael Maltus, a graduate of England's Emerson College, well-known center for bio-intensive gardening, designed the four-acre kitchen garden, which ultimately will be a ten-acre farm. The land is intensively planted with over 1,500 kinds of vegetables, fruits, and herbs. The residue from grape crushing at Fetzer Vineyards is mixed with compost to make a rich fertilizer and top-dressing for the garden. Plans include the addition of free-range chicken, game bird, and rabbit pens.

In its first two years the garden produced impressive crops of organically grown vegetables, including unusual and old varieties. Raspberries, strawberries, nectarines, and apricots recently have been planted, and some already have produced fruit. Several varieties of apples, some espaliered, with flowers and herbs underneath, were planted European-style at forty-five degree angles so that leafy canopies shade fruit from hot summer sun. Artichokes, amaranth (with drooping seeds said to be twice as rich nutritionally as wheat), and asparagus beds also have been established.

An array of fragrant herbs is interplanted with flowers. Unusual black-flowered pansies, French marigolds, double-ruffled pinks, and alyssum are mixed with basil (cinnamon variety is spicy on the tongue), thyme, oregano, and many other herbs. Straw flowers are dried for winter use on tables at the winery's Sundial Grill in Hopland. Fruit, vegetables, and flowers (including edible blossoms) are used in the restaurant year round.

A pavilion with test kitchens, overlooking a small lake, is used for food tastings, for Fetzer food and wine reports, and as a site for visiting chefs to participate in demonstrations and forums.

Wisteria drapes an old farm cottage, and fall crops of spinach, French lettuces, chard, and broccoli come up beside ripening squash and pumpkins. In a courtyard between the old buildings beds of penstemons, petunias, and geraniums, olive trees, and a fountain add to the atmosphere of fruitful abundance.

*Fan palm and impatiens make an unusual combination*

**Getting There:** Highway 101 north of Santa Rosa to Hopland; exit east on Highway 175 and go about half a mile. At the curve, go straight ahead to elm-lined driveway of Valley Oaks (a small peaked-roof building marks the entrance). Park in lot.

**Admission:** Free. By appointment (707) 744-1298.

**Facilities:** Restrooms, benches, picnic tables, drinking fountains. Handicapped access good. Bed-and-breakfast Valley Oaks Inn was created from an 1890s barn; grape arbor picnic grounds accommodate 400 people; meeting rooms by reservation. Demonstrations and seminars in pavilion.

**Nearby:** Fetzer Vineyards wine tasting and sales, delicatessen, and restaurant are in Hopland at the intersection of Highways 101 and 175. Hopland Brewery, Thatcher Hotel (built in 1880), and many antique shops are on Main Street.

# Mendocino Coast Botanical Gardens

❀ 18220 North Highway 1, Fort Bragg

This seventeen-acre garden, operated by a non-profit organization for the Mendocino Coast Recreation and Park District, displays several thousand kinds of native and cultivated plants that do well in the cool, mild-winter climate of the Mendocino coast. Major collections include hybrid, species, and dwarf rhododendrons, dwarf conifers, heathers, perennials, ivies, drought-tolerant plants, heritage roses, and camellias. The garden is sheltered by a native pine forest, which is home to many birds, deer, and small wildlife. A year-round creek flows through a fern-covered canyon, and there is a rocky intertidal habitat at the water's edge.

The gardens were developed in the early 1960s by Ernest Schoefer, a retired nurseryman, and his wife Betty. While clearing, building trails, and planting the property, the Schoefers discovered an old house in the undergrowth and a family cemetery in the pine forest; the house was restored and the cemetery preserved. Cleared brush was piled in windrows and allowed to decompose, then the compost was returned to the soil at planting time, a practice that was consistently followed as the gardens were established.

The perennial garden near the entrance has curving swaths of lawn separated by beds and mounds filled with plants in unusual combinations. The extensive heather collection shows interesting textures and gradations of green, with some plants turning rusty brown in fall. A rock garden has creeping and rambling plants, including shrubby and groundcovering rock roses and low-growing helianthemums with brightly colored flowers. There is even a garden of succulents and cacti.

Plants for shade include native wild ginger with heart-shaped leaves and bell-like flowers, native sword ferns, and lily-of-the-valley. Along winding paths in filtered light an astonishing variety of rhododendrons command attention, especially in peak bloom in April and May. Where two paths meet, unusual big-leaf rhododendrons with leathery leaves grow under tanbark oaks. Pacific wax myrtles with picturesque trunks shade ferns and native irises. Monterey cypresses and shore pines (*Pinus contorta*) line the ocean headlands trail. Sounds of surf and foghorns draw visitors on to dramatic views of the ocean.

A trail in the fern canyon is sun-dappled and quiet. Pines, oaks, alders, and redwoods grow along the creek, where bridges, small rapids, and waterfalls make this a popular area for children. Trails back to the demonstration garden pass from shady glens through sunny, open areas, providing a shifting display of azaleas

*Rhododendrons, azaleas, and foxgloves along woodland path*

and columbines, Persian lilies, foxgloves, daylilies, and sages. This is a garden for all seasons; something is almost always in bloom.

**Getting There:** Highway 1 six miles north of Mendocino, two miles south of Ft. Bragg. Park in lot.

**Admission:** Adults, $4; seniors, $3; children 12 and under, free. Open daily 9am to 5pm. Group discounts. Reservations required for group tours.

**Facilities:** Restrooms, benches, drinking fountain, picnic tables. Handicapped access on main trails only; side trails unsurfaced. No dogs. Retail nursery with special plant sales in April and October. List of nearby rhododendron and specialty nurseries available. Lawn area available for weddings and events. Call (707) 964-4352 for information.

**Nearby:** Garden Cafe, next door but not affiliated with Botanical Gardens, is open daily 8am to 4pm. The ocean is about half a mile away.

# Also of Interest

**Bamboo Sorcery Nursery,** 666 Wagnon Road, Sebastopol (707) 823-5866. Hundreds of rare and unusual varieties of bamboo in a hilly setting among redwood trees. Informative annual catalog. Visit by appointment.

**Fort Ross State Historic Park**, gardens at Call House, 19005 Coast Highway 1, Jenner (707) 847-3286. Around old farmhouse near historic fort are gardens planted around 1900, with old roses, datura, geraniums, princess flower, and other plants.

**Lone Pine Gardens Nursery**, 6450 Lone Pine Lane, Sebastopol (707) 823-5024. Extensive collection of bonsai, from seedlings to specimen plants; unusual grasses, dwarf conifers, bamboo, cacti, and succulents.

*Mature plants at Bamboo Sorcery*

**McAllister Water Gardens Nursery**, 7420 St. Helena Highway, Yountville (707) 944-0921. Open March through September. Waterlilies, ornamental grasses, pond plants, flowering perennials, Japanese irises; information about culture of water plants. Catalog.

**Neon Palm Nursery**, 1560 Sebastopol Road, Santa Rosa (707) 578-7467. Hardy subtropical plants; unusual and rare indoor and outdoor palms; some other plants, unusual trees; informative, attractive catalog.

**Smith & Hawken**, 35 Corte Madera, Mill Valley (415) 381-0279. Beautiful catalog of fine garden equipment, garden furniture, and unusual items; small, specialized nursery with herbs, perennials, unusual trees; fine demonstration garden; second store in Stanford Shopping Center, Palo Alto (415) 321-0403.

**Urban Tree Farm**, 4871 Old Redwood Highway, Santa Rosa (707) 542-3166. Full-service six-acre nursery specializing in container trees; many large espaliered trees, vines, and shrubs; fruit trees; information center with books, landscape guides.

**Vallejo Home**, West Spain and West Third streets, Sonoma (707) 938-1578. Restored mid-nineteenth-century home and chalet (now a museum) of General Mariano Guadalupe Vallejo; attractive gardens with some original trees.

**Wildwood Farm Nursery**, 10300 Sonoma Highway, Kenwood, and second location at Glen Ellen Grist Mill Road, Glen Ellen (707) 833-1161. Hardy perennials, collectible plants, California natives, many hostas, ferns, native oaks.

**Wishing Well Nursery & Antiques**, 306 Bohemian Highway, Freestone, west of Sebastopol (707) 823-3710. Quaint bridge to pond with black swans, geese, ducks; roses, Japanese maples, fuchsias, begonias, deciduous trees, bromeliads, antique shop.

# Seasonal Trips for Special Enjoyment

Most gardens in Northern California are at their best in mid-spring, but some specialize in plants that bloom earlier in the year, while others, such as rose gardens, are most colorful in summer. The exact months in which spring or summer may be said to arrive varies not only year to year but by location. Temperatures generally are milder near the coast — warmer in winter and cooler in summer — and this has an effect on plant growth and on flowering.

Even the low hills near San Francisco Bay have a remarkable effect not only on winter rainfall but on temperature. In summer Walnut Creek may have temperatures of one hundred degrees, while less than fifteen miles away in Berkeley the temperature may be in the seventies. In winter the pattern is reversed: the east side of

the Berkeley hills may have ten degrees of frost, while around the bay temperatures are well above freezing. The Central Valley is both colder in winter and hotter in summer than closer to the coast, and in the Sierra foothills there may be snow on the ground while San Francisco is well on its way into spring.

This makes it difficult to specify the months in which a particular garden can be expected to be at its best, especially if visitors are most interested in flowers. In much of Northern California April and May could be said to be mid-spring, and the months of June through August are summer in almost all parts of the region. The cool, rainy seasons of fall and winter typically begin in October and continue through February or March, though in dry years the rains may be over by December. In unirrigated gardens or natural areas flowering depends heavily on the amount and timing of rains. In cultivated gardens plants respond mainly to day length and temperature. If you want to be certain that plants are in bloom, it is best to call the garden in question before planning a visit. Many garden enthusiasts, however, appreciate the beauty of plants in and out of leaf and flower and find skillfully designed gardens pleasing in all seasons.

Although in Northern California's winter-wet, summer-dry Mediterranean climate some plants will be flowering at almost any time of year, gardens and nurseries for winter visiting generally include those with strong underlying design (including formal gardens, Japanese gardens, and gardens with considerable architectural detail) or those in which trees, evergreen or not, are a main feature. Gardens for fall visits include those with colorful berries or trees with good autumn leaf color, such as ginkgoes, Japanese maples, and liquidambars. With such observations in mind, the following suggestions are offered for seasonal trips to gardens mentioned in this book. Directions to the gardens can be found in the text.

**Spring:**

*San Francisco/Peninsula:*

Strybing Arboretum
Japanese Tea Garden
Grace Marchant Garden
Acres of Orchids
Central Park Japanese Garden
Filoli
Yerba Buena Nursery
Edgewood Park
Gamble Garden Center

*Oakland/East Bay:*

Blake Garden
Tilden Park Botanic Garden
U.C. Botanical Garden

*San Jose/South Bay:*

Hakone Japanese Garden
Villa Montalvo
Kelley Park Japanese Garden

*Santa Cruz/Monterey Bay:*

Lester Rowntree Arboretum
John Ewing Orchids

*Central Valley/Gold Country:*

U.C. Davis Arboretum
Capitol Park
Daffodil Hill
Shannon-Knox House

*North Bay/Mendocino:*

Old St. Hilary's
Iron Horse Vineyards
Sonoma Horticultural Nursery
Mendocino Coast Botanical Gardens

**Summer:**

*San Francisco/Peninsula:*

Grace Marchant Garden
Sunset Magazine
Allied Arts Guild

*Oakland/East Bay:*

Blake Garden
Berkeley Rose Garden
Tilden Park Botanic Garden
U.C. Botanical Garden
East Bay Garden Center
Morcom Amphitheater of Roses
Kaiser Center Roof Garden

*San Jose/South Bay:*

San Jose Rose Garden
Rosicrucian Park
Hecker Pass Family Adventure
Goldsmith Seeds

*Santa Cruz/Monterey Bay:*

Antonelli Brothers Begonias
Roses of Yesterday and Today
Old Monterey
Tor House
Carmel Valley Begonia Gardens

*Central Valley/Gold Country:*

Fountain Square Nursery
Bourn Cottage

*North Bay/Mendocino:*

John's Rose Garden
Garden Valley Ranch
Korbel Winery

**Fall:**

*San Jose/South Bay:*

Saso Herb Gardens
Overfelt Gardens

*Central Valley/Gold Country:*

Micke Grove Japanese Garden
Auburn Library
King's Mums

*North Bay/Mendocino:*

Marin Art and Garden Center
Ira Cook House
Napa Valley Wineries
Great Petaluma Desert Nursery
A Sticky Business
Luther Burbank Gardens
Fetzer's Valley Oaks

**Winter:**

*San Francisco/Peninsula:*

Japanese Tea Garden
Conservatory of Flowers
Acres of Orchids
Rodin Sculpture Garden

*Oakland/East Bay:*

Tilden Park Botanic Garden
Dunsmuir House
Tao House
John Muir House

*San Jose/South Bay:*

Hakone Japanese Garden
Rosicrucian Park
Kelley Park Japanese Garden

*Santa Cruz/Monterey Bay:*

U.C. Santa Cruz Arboretum

*Central Valley/Gold Country:*

Capitol Park
Micke Grove Japanese Garden
Chinese Temple Garden

*North Bay/Mendocino:*

Miniature Plant Kingdom
Bamboo Sorcery
Kyoto Koi & Garden Center
Neon Palm Nursery

# Index